# ADOPTED LIKE ME

## *Chosen to Search for Truth, Identity, and a Birthmother*

## Michael C. Watson

Gallery of Diamonds
Publishing

# ADOPTED LIKE ME
### *Chosen to Search for Truth, Identity, and a Birthmother*
Michael C. Watson

## Gallery of Diamonds
### Publishing
2915 Redhill Avenue • Suite G-102
Costa Mesa, CA 92626 U.S.A.

www.galleryofdiamonds.com

© 2005 by Michael C. Watson. First Printing
Based on original edition © 1998 In Search of Mom – Journey of an Adoptee.

Also by Michael C. Watson:
*In Search of Mom – Journey of an Adoptee*
*Why Mom Deserves a Diamond™ - Twelve Years of Love*
*Why Mom Deserves a Diamond™ - The Legendary Contest*
*Why Mom Deserves a Diamond™ - 10th Anniversary of the Greatest Contest on Earth*
*Why Mom Deserves a Diamond™ - The Greatest Contest on Earth*
*Why Mom Deserves a Diamond™ - A Millennium Mother's Day Tribute*
*Why Mom Deserves a Diamond™ - Seventh Anniversary Edition*
*Why Mom Deserves a Diamond™ - 1,500 Essay Winners for 1998*
*Why Mom Deserves a Diamond™ - 1,002 Essay Winners for 1997*
*Why Mom Deserves a Diamond™ - 732 Essay Winners for 1996*
*Why Mom Deserves a Diamond™ - 391 Essay Winners for 1995*
*Why Mom Deserves a Diamond™ - 1994 Essay Winners*
*Why Mom Deserves a Diamond™ - 1993 Essay Winners*

**Library of Congress Catalog Card Number: 2004096175**
**ISBN 1-891665-36-7**

Copies of **Adopted Like Me** may be ordered directly from the publisher for **$14.95** plus $3.95 for shipping (California residents add 7.75% sales tax.) For terms in volume quantities, please contact the publisher.

Book Cover and Design by Claudio Canestro.
Cover: Gualan, Guatemala. Heaven's Gift™ cameo by OTC International.

# Table of Contents

# *Acknowledgements*

Thanks to:

My Mom, Martha Velia Watson, the only mother I have ever known. Thank you for your courage in allowing me to search for my beginnings. I love you because you first loved me.

Jean Paton, 1907-2002. Founder of Orphan Voyage and the Mother of Adoption Reform. Thank you for your courage in speaking out for adoptee's rights by questioning sealed adoption records.

My beautiful wife, Maria del Carmen, who understood my compelling force. My daughters Adela Patricia and Michaela Maria.

My extraordinary staff who helped perpetuate the legendary Why Mom Deserves a Diamond™ contest. To establish a nationwide tribute of this magnitude has required extreme dedication. They have shared my vision in making it the greatest contest on earth; Sandra Babic, Claudio Canestro, Jo Christian, Maria Claypool, Wayne Cleary, Sandy Fredlund, Pam Gomez, Mac Malan, Terry and Carmen Ogles, Chuong Pham and Kerry Schofield.

All of the 140,000 students that have thus far submitted their Mother's writings.

The gemstone winners--it has been an honor to meet you and your mothers. Listening to you recite your words of love has made us all better persons.

Sandra Babic and Willene DeGroot for editing this book.

The mystery lady who sent me anonymous letters of advice.

My good friends Daniel, Brad, Touraj, Shlomo, Walt, Eric, Cameron, Craig, Pastor Tom, Pastor Bill, Pastor Ron, and Dorothy Jean.

My *new* relatives Grandma Hattie, Uncle David, Aunt Joy Lee, Aunt Mary Jane, Uncle Louie and Cousin Michael. My siblings Michael David, Kenny Ray and Susie. And Debra Kay, wherever you are.

The authors for their extraordinary essays. Listed in alphabetical order by last name, they are: Tami Adams, Tiffany Allen, Sneha Antani, Karena Arreola, Michael Baello, Nghiem Banh, Justin Bareis, Katie Bruce, Connor Bryan, Tyler Buttle, Laura Cataldi, Glenda Cea, Kathleen Choi, Leon Lin Chung, Richard Cinco, Logan Cluttey, Alyssa Connella, Robert Crabbs, Lindsey Croft, Lauren Cruz, Michael Cumpian, Dalton, Megan Ashley Darakjian, E. J. Debowski, R. Adam Diaz, John Dinh, Regan Doyle, Justin Duarte, Michael Ducharm, Travis Dziad, Sandy Enriquez, April Evans, Nicole Feinour, Dante Ferri  Kalynn Fowler, Robin Gibbons, Jacob Gissinger, Dawn Glaves, Ashley Goodell, Robert Gread, Jennifer Hagen, Erica Haggerty, Zavina Hartley, Michele Helget, Nikki Hernandez, Jesus Hernandez Jr., Dominique Hilsabeck, Becky Hindt, Lauren Hopkins, Marian Hsieh, Harry Hudson, Jessica Hulce, Megan Hutchinson, Alissa Isenberg, Bryan Ives, Joree Jacobs, Naomi Johnson, Alyssa Jordan, Ann Kang, Albert Kazi, Timmy Kelemen, Margaret Ketchersid, Christyn Keyes, Priya Khanijou, Lauren Kiang,

Paula Kim, Scott Kircher, Jason Kirstein, Amy Kjose, Julia Koller-Nielson, Ashley Kreidler, Jackie Kuhns, Jeff Lai, Tiffany Lamanski, Yuri Lara, Joseph Lee, Lindsey Linker, Jennifer MacKintosh, Aregnaz Malakyan, Adrianna Martinez, Kelly Mc Lachlan, Katie Merrill, Richard Miller, Amy Moore, Ryan Moore, Alison Murphy, Martin C. O' Toole, Lauren M. O'Hara, Chris Olsen-Phillips, Rashika Patel, Janelle Patterson, Blair Perkins, Jennifer Plankenhorn, Laura Poladian, Rio Ponce, Niranjan Ramadas, Tawnya Ravy, Jennifer Reed, Diana Relth, Catherine Riddick, Ruth Ringenberg, Ian Ringgenburg, Ashley Robinson, Meredith Rogerson, Monica Ross, Katie Ruffalo, Roberto Ruiz, Ryan Russell, Eric Rygh, Johnathan Sanders, Brielle Saracini, Caitlin Schafer, Cortneee Schlabach, Jessica Schultz, Matthew W. Scott, Jennifer Scruggs, Sarah Sharaf, Aris Simsarian, Genevieve Slunka, Sammi Smith, Ryan Stephenson, Cathleen Streicher, Erin Swanson, Momo Takahashi, Victor Taylor, Carly Thomas, Rachel Tomberlin, Brice Tomlinson, Katie Truesdell, My Truong, Andrea Van Deusen, Michelle Vu, Amanda Wheeler, Khadija Yakub, Lily Yang, Pauline Yee, and Alexandra Zagorski.

Due to legal advice, a few names have been changed. I sincerely apologize for those who would want their identities revealed, after all, that is one purpose of this book, to heal the plague, called Secrets, that is familiar to most adoptees.

There are so many people responsible for this book. Please forgive me if you do not see your name listed.

*"Life is not a particular place or a destination. Life is a path. To be able to stop pursuing the future allows us to realize that all the wonderful things we seek are present in us, in the present moment."*

**Our Appointment With Life: Discourse on Living Happily in the Present Moment. Thich Nhat Hahn. Permission of Parallax Press, Berkeley, California.**

# *Preface*

The life of an adoptee is sometimes like that of an ancient voyager who searches for the unknown. The explorers, however, used navigational tools and the stars to guide their destiny. They had their sights on the wonders that lay ahead of them. An adoptee, on the other hand, travels in the opposite direction.

The adoptee searches for the past. Therefore, he or she cannot rely on sophisticated equipment or the constellations, but rather on hope and perseverance. The map of the past is many times derived from faint clues that one has heard or seen.

I am a prehistoric time traveler -- an astronaut of the past. I am adopted.

Perhaps we share the same circumstance. According to the first report on adopted children by the 2000 US Census Bureau, there are currently five to six million adoptees (about one in fifty) in the United States.

I was born February 25, 1958. The name on my original birth certificate simply said "infant", but was changed three days later to the name I have owned ever since. All the traces of my ancestry were stripped away. I had no bloodroots and the branches of my family tree ascended into nothingness. Life before I exited a womb never existed. There was nothing genetically connected to me or a face that resembled me.

My past had been deleted.

In essence, my identity died on February 28, 1958, when an invisible hand switched the blueprint for my life. My adoptive parents, on the other hand, were given life, for I brought an immeasurable joy that was no different from the elation demonstrated by any biological parents.

In changing only a couple of letters, *adoptee* becomes *amputee*. The definitions are amazingly similar, for each implies that a piece of an individual that was once inherent has been wholly dismembered. For many adoptees, it is the limbs of history that have been severed.

In reality, by the laws of the court, I was re-born. Some adoptees have the sensation of a second birth. Others despair from being denied any birth. My original birth certificate and adoption proceedings became forever *sealed* in a tightly guarded file.

The documentation of my life began on February 28, 1958. My proud adoptive mother can show you photos of me on that date. From that moment on I would travel through time at the same speed as anyone else.

But there would be no road behind me.

As an adoptee, it is difficult to comprehend the feelings of an adoptive parent. Likewise, one cannot pretend to experience the feelings of a birthparent who has relinquished a child. I do hope to enrich the reader by unveiling the emotions that possess many adoptees like me who have lived or continue to live in the world of ancestral bewilderment.

Some may say that they know an adoptee who has no desire to uncover his or her biological roots. I can't help thinking that there is an underlying hunger in every adoptee to know his or her origin in the cosmos. Some adoptees take many years before they are ready to search. Others never attempt. But I believe the yearning is still there, however dormant. One adoptee said,

"Adoption is like walking into a movie theatre and the movie has already started. You enjoy the movie very much and applaud at the end, but you still want to see the beginning."

An adoptee's longing to find his or her roots should not be interpreted as a lack of devotion to the adoptive parents. In many cases, it is a psychological journey to find oneself. The American Adoption Congress says, "Searching is not about finding a different life. It is about discovering the truth of your very existence." It takes emotional security for adoptive parents not to feel threatened and incredible strength to offer support. Many adoptees have recognized a stronger relationship with their adoptive parents after reunions or contacts with birthparents.

I am one author who agrees that one's birthright should be an unconditional human gift. After learning the truth of their births, no matter what the circumstances, most adoptees have experienced an emotional release. The pages of the past reveal where one has been and are stepping-stones to the present.

The sociologist Peter Berger said, "Unlike puppets, we have the possibility of stopping in our movements, looking up and perceiving the machinery by which we have been moved. In this act lies the first step toward freedom." Although the reference was about one's socially stratified state, I now see the words differently.

The puppets are those adoptees who live in the illusion that their adoptive parents are their "real" parents. They have symbolically erased their birthparents from their consciousness and have completely removed them from the map of their being. I am puzzled by those adoptees who are afraid to inquire into the origination of their making, for they sometimes live in deliberate darkness their entire lives.

The machinery is the probate court, the placing attorney, the physician at the time of birth, and the adoption agencies. It is the entire adoption system, from when the birthmother first signs the order of relinquishment to when the social worker makes periodic visits to the adoptive parent's home.

And finally, the freedom is the closure that the adoptee obtains from learning the most basic truth most of us take for granted -- our origin.

There will be uncounted adoptees who will never unravel the mystery of their ancestry. Other adoptees will never know their heritage simply because they refused to look. Still others may have an ardent passion but few clues to follow.

It would be intriguing to find out how an individual would be different if history could be changed; if one were given different surroundings, if one were raised by biological instead of adoptive parents, and vice versa. Although heredity is the main determinant of one's physical traits, I am quite certain that my adoptive parents and everyone I have interacted with on my journey have shaped the person I am today. I am who I am because of who you are. My wonder and curiosity, along with my understanding of love and life's purpose, is the result of my journey.

Although my path was filled with disappointments, that joyous moment of reunion will forever echo in my brain. As I flew back home to Southern California, I resounded with inspiration. Far above the clouds I began scribbling words on scrap paper. The final result was this book.

Life's complexities and sufferings can yield great strengths. The wonderful consequence of my lifelong quest has been the *Why Mom Deserves a Diamond*™ contest. With the help of my family and staff, it has strengthened the bonds between countless children and their mothers across the country. Since the inception of the contest, over 140,000 kids have expressed their words of love for their moms. The contest has reached millions, and everyone it has touched has benefited. The chain reaction is wonderful; when kids know they are loved, they love themselves. When they love themselves, they love others. When one loves others, the world becomes our safe and beautiful home.

> *"My mom is as sweet as an apple, and I love her very much and so hard that I can't even forget her. Doesn't matter how big she is or how small she is—I still love her."*
>
> **Michaela Maria Watson, at age 4 1/2.**

*From the whole world, I chose you as my own.*

# PART ONE
# The Journey

*Rafiki the baboon came walking toward him. "If you want to see your father again, look down there," Rafiki said, pointing into the pool of water next to them.  Simba saw the face of his father staring back at him.  "You see?" Rafiki said.  "He lives in you."*

**The Lion King.** Disney Enterprises.

# 1. Primal Beginnings

I always knew I was adopted. That was never a secret. Mom used to call me her little *adopted angel*. I felt special because I was *chosen*. Dad told me that they picked me out from a large room filled with cribs of babies. After seeing me in the middle of the room, he said, "I'll take that curly-headed one over there!" Mom told me that before I was born her arms would ache with envy every time she saw a mother holding a baby.

My mom could not bear a child. After a few years of correspondence with a lawyer, a call came saying I was born, was a male, and could be adopted. Mom and Dad drove to Indianapolis, signed the necessary papers, and returned south to the home where I would be raised -- New Albany. The small, sleepy town in Indiana was mostly a white Methodist community that lay on the north bank of the Ohio River, peering across to its larger neighbor, Louisville.

I was the talk of the town and some confused neighbors said they didn't even know Mom was pregnant. Nevertheless, on that day, Mrs. Watson became a mother. By trial and error, she learned the correct amount of blankets to cover me and the safest way to secure my diaper with a pin. I never tasted mother's milk, but was prescribed a stinky mixture made from soybeans. My complexion was olive; my parents were fair-skinned. My hair was dark and coiled; my parents' hair was straight. Neighbors enjoyed guessing what I looked like. Some said Italian.

Mom's name was Martha Velia. Somehow the nickname "Micky" stuck with close friends. And for whatever reason, Dad called her "Veeler," disfiguring her name even more. I remembered her as plump, gracious, and quite attractive. She could gain complete friendship and trust with anyone she met and could also dissolve any argument between friends with caring words and tender solutions. I always thought of her as an extreme worrier and tried to make her see the more serene side of life. She kept a spotless house, re-painted each room a different color every two years, and hung clothes on a tight wire suspended between two mulberry trees in the back yard long after most neighbors had more efficient ways of drying garments.

Dad was a tall, thin man named Stoy. He finished only the seventh grade and worked long hours as a pipe fitter until his retirement. He had a hard life and, like many people living in America during the Great Depression, was more concerned with economic survival than even the most primal luxuries. He and Mom got along fine when he wasn't drinking. He smoked stinky smelling Tareyton's and then changed to a pipe. He was the only man I ever knew who could take a drag from a cigarette so deep that smoke would pour out of his mouth after the third exhale. The sun-filled living room was always infiltrated with horizontal layers of blue-gray smoke that would hover motionless unless a breeze came through.

I remember our three-story house. I miss the creaks of its wooden floors, the oversized bathtub, and the panoramic view of mature maples and gentle hills from our back porch. I used the upstairs attic for dreaming and throwing darts at monsters I had crayoned on the cardboard-thin walls. We rented the downstairs

1947.
Author's adoptive parents.
Stoy Edward Watson: 1916-1995,
and Martha.

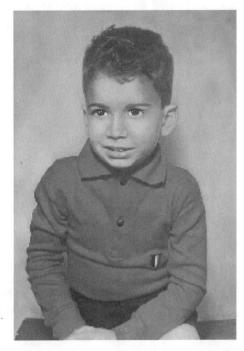

Author at three years old.

to various occupants. The middle layer was where my parents spent most of their lives.

Mom and I would always eat in the kitchen. She delivered Dad's dinner on an aluminum tray, and he would eat in the living room while watching television. In a blend between serious and playful, he would always refer to Mom's cooking as garbage. He had an acute sense of smell and cautiously sniffed everything before inserting it into his mouth.

"Veeler! Whar's my garbage?" he would protest from the living room sofa.

"I'm coming, Stoy, just hold yer horses!" she would yell from the kitchen. Mom would run to the rescue, spread Dad's dinner on the coffee table like a waitress in a fine restaurant, and return to the kitchen.

I always wondered why Mom was so subservient to my Dad, and theorized it was a mixture of respect and fear. Mainly the latter. Our supper menu never seemed to vary: pinto beans with a strip of jowl bacon, fried potatoes, and corn bread.

### Who am I?

Mom always had the remarkable ability to know when something was wrong, and sometimes I wondered if she could telepathically read my thoughts. Either I was thinking aloud or she noticed I was more quiet than usual, but one time she came in my bedroom and sat on my bed.

"Where did I *really* come from?" I asked. "Do you know who my *real* mother is?" Mom comforted me in her beautiful way by grabbing my hand and pulling me down beside her. She concluded for the hundredth time that she and Dad were my *real* parents because they picked me out specially.

At ten going on eleven, I didn't settle for that answer anymore.

"Where did I *come* from?" I demanded more seriously, stressing a different word. "Who was my *mother*?"

"Stoy, honey?" she projected her voice around the hallway. "Would you come in here for a minute?" The bedsprings cringed from our weight.

Dad's face appeared from around the corner. He had an unusually earnest expression from Mom's imploring tone.

"Whaddaya want, Veeler?"

"Michael wants to know about his birthmother."

"Well, tell him," he said.

Both of them stared at each other for a few seconds waiting for the other to speak. Dad spoke first.

"Your mother's name was Betty Price. She was twenty-two years old when she had you. You were born at Community Hospital in Indianapolis. That's all we know, Mi-kel. If we knew anymore, we would tell you, but that's all we know." His voice was sincere with a shaky authority.

"Who was my father?" I continued, before completely absorbing the first answer.

"All it said on your birth certificate was, 'father unknown'. Maybe she didn't want to give his name... we'll never know," Dad answered. " And that's all we know, Mi-kel. All you need to know is that we love you more than anything in this world and that's all you need to know."

And with that final proclamation he returned to the living room.

I turned toward Mom again. Her expression was the same as when I asked her about the birds and the bees. For many years the secret was "the birds *fly* and the bees *buzz*." Later, she proceeded to tell me the truth, in adult language, and the whole idea of creating babies was unsettling.

"Michael, like we have always told you since you were old enough to hear, we adopted you when you were three days old. We wanted to have a baby so badly..." She paused, realizing she wasn't really answering my questions. "Just a minute." She got up, went to her bedroom, made some clanging sounds from an old tin box that she and Dad kept in their closet, and returned with a handful of papers. "Here. You can have these, Michael," she said, handing me three flimsy documents with dirty blue covers.

I carefully unfolded the one on top. It was labeled: *Decree of Adoption.* It was typed on wrinkly, onionskin paper and almost disintegrated in my hands. I did an eyeball review of the parchment. Other than the legal jargon, I did see the name Betty Price typed in several blanks. The other two blue documents were titled, *Petition for Custody of Child* and *Order.* They seemed like the same thing, but with Betty Price's name typed in different blanks.

My life force drained as I sat dumbfounded. If Betty Price was my *real* mother, then who were these people, I wondered? The thought of being chosen was not special anymore. I just wanted to be regular. The abstract word, adopted, began to take on the form of an unearthly silhouette.

"Why did my mother give me up?" I asked bravely.

"Honey, maybe she couldn't afford to keep you. Maybe she was unmarried and didn't have enough money to support you."

My stomach ached. Was adoption good or bad? Should I have been proud or ashamed? I surely didn't feel that this was a fortunate circumstance, and realized that being adopted meant that someone originally rejected me. For years to come, the condition of being adopted would no longer be a joy, but rather a Scarlet "A" that would be stamped forever into my consciousness.

"We got you through a private attorney, Michael. His name was Raymond Demaree. He was the nicest old man, Michael. I'll never forget those black olives he gave us when we signed the papers. We ate them right there at his desk. The doctor who delivered you was Dr. William Fitzgerald. He was an old man also. Here," she continued, handing me a crinkled postcard. "This is where you were born. I saved it for you."

The postcard was a photograph of Community Hospital. The building was rather drab, with no trees surrounding the pale brick structure. Scribbled on the back was Mom's handwriting, 'Where Michael was born.' I couldn't believe it. She must have planned on giving me these papers since the day I was born. She had waited until that special time--today. Then she handed me another paper. It was the actual bill that my parents paid for my birthmother's three-day stay at the hospital. It read,

Community Hospital
Patient:        Betty Price.
Room No.        240W
Date:           February 27, 1958
Age:            22
Address:        2115 N. Delaware Street, Indianapolis

North Delaware Street. I fantasized about her still living there. What did she look like, I wondered?

"Did you ever see my mother?" I asked.

"I could have, I guess," she answered. "She was probably still in the recovery room when we went to get you. She was the farthest thing from our minds, because it wasn't her we wanted; it was *you*."

I felt like crying from the emotion and confusion, but held it inside.

"Oh, here. Take this. " she said as she unfolded another piece of paper. "Mr. Demaree gave this beautiful poem to us when we signed the adoption papers. Those olives were so delicious."

I read the anonymous poem.

### To An Adopted Child

*Dear, do not weep*
*By every act of mine I am your mother*
*By my sleepless nights*
*By every step in the long day's design*
*By the clear gaze*
*By all your care in your beginning days*
*Your warm, soft body held against my breast*
*Comforted me and dried  my disappointed tears*
*You made a real home of our lonely nest*

*Now we look forward to the fruitful years*
*With you beside us bearing in your hands*
*The love that every mother's heart demands*
*Though you may not be flesh of my flesh*
*Our love goes deeper still*
*I am your mother by the power of will*
*Because I did not want to walk alone*
*From the whole world, I chose you for my own*

"We love you, Michael. You were the greatest thing that had ever happened to me and your daddy. Just because Betty Price gave birth to you doesn't make her your mother. I took care of you when you were sick, made you lunch every day for school, and put a Band-Aid on your knee every time you fell." She smiled, gave me an unusually tight hug, and went back to the kitchen.

I didn't ask any more questions.

*"Ask and it will be given to you; seek and you will find; knock and the door will be opened to you."*
**Jesus of Nazareth.**

## 2. First Search

The resolution to find my birthmother came when I was
seventeen. I hungered to find out who she was and
therefore who I was. Now was my chance, I thought, to
find the identity of my origin. I was tired of telling people "I
don't know" whenever asked about my nationality. "What are you,
Michael? Jewish? Greek?" Then they would say, "What do you
mean, *you don't know?* What is your mother?"

"I don't know that either," I would say defeated.

"Who is your father?" they always prodded further.

"I don't know," I would continue stupidly. "I was adopted. I
really don't know who or what I am."

Then the same story would unfold that I had told a thousand
times. So many people just didn't understand what it was like
not knowing their mother or father or brother or sister. Being
left-handed, I also never knew what it was like to write with my
right hand, but that handicap never made me feel as cheated as the
denial of my birthright.

I had my driver's license now. I was free. I had kept the adoption
records that Mom had given me as a child. The address rang in my
head -- 2115 North Delaware. I vowed to myself that I must go there.

What would I do after I arrived? What if my birthmother
was still living there? What would I say, "Hi, Mom, I'm home?"
Could I ever address her with such a sacred title that I had only

vocalized to the woman who nurtured me ever since I was three days old? I began to think of every conceivable danger associated with this sort of quest. What if she were married and never told her husband about me? What if she had other children? I could destroy her marriage and her life.

The fear of the adventure almost became too great for me. Mom was not prepared when I told her my decision. I really do not think she could understand why anyone would want to seek answers to such questions if they had wonderful adoptive parents.

I decided that maybe a personal letter would be a good solution. After much thought I wrote:

Dear Mom,

I know how you feel when I ask questions about being adopted. I'm not searching for new parents. I just need to know where I came from. I've never met anybody who has even looked like me, and sometimes I feel strange.

I know you told me that it is the people who raise you who are your real parents, and you have cared for me more than any mother I have ever known. I just want to know the truth.

I'm driving to Indianapolis. If I find my birthmother, please don't think that I'll forget about you. I know you are my mother.

I love you.

The next morning I placed the note face up on the kitchen table and left at dawn. The day before I had purchased a gold-plated necklace from a gift shop. It would be a token for my birthmother and symbolize that I did not have hard feelings. After all, she had given me the gift of life. The abstract amulet had two graceful curves, representing her and myself. The larger curve seemed to "give birth" to the smaller one, which met each other at the bottom.  If she didn't want any further contact, then she could still keep the necklace as a reminder that I am a part of her.

The outskirts of Indianapolis came into view at about seven a.m. Although the northbound drive on Highway 65 was a peaceful one, I soon became tightly sandwiched between rushing vehicles.  One hundred miles seemed like a terribly long distance to drive by oneself, especially after just receiving a license and an old blue Chevy Biscayne. As I jockeyed for space, I wondered if all the cars were beeping at me.

Miraculously, I found the *North Delaware* sign.   I slowly crept through the calm street lined with large old houses and leafy trees on either side.  It looked like a dilapidated neighborhood that probably was a very nice place back in 1958.  I saw 2111, 2113, and... nothing.  There was no house at 2115!  It was a vacant lot.  I backed up to see if I missed something, but there was no such address. After curbing the Biscayne, I sauntered to where the house was supposed to be.  The early morning air whisked by coolly on my bare arms.  I saw only damp and warped wooden boards that lay criss-cross where a house used to be.

This was the *Twilight Zone*, I thought, stomping around on the ground where my birthmother had once strolled.  There was a mail carrier walking at a fast pace along the street.  I stopped him and asked if he ever knew a Betty Price who used to live there.  He replied, "I've been on this route for many years.  Hmm... I think I remember a Betty Price, but it was so long ago.  Sorry, sir."

Off I went, trudging up and down the street knocking on every door.  The first house was empty.  The next occupant shuffled inside, then briefly peeked through the curtains, but refused to answer.  Another neighbor said she had just moved there two weeks prior and didn't know anybody.

I managed to find the county building, and was directed to an elevator reaching Probate Judge Jameson's office.  I entered his suite and was greeted by a balding, stout man who motioned for me from his large chair. I introduced myself, told him that I was adopted, and said I wanted to find my birthmother. The judge paused for a few seconds to find the right words. "Adoptees come here all the time, Mr. Watson. They all want to know who their mothers are and where they came from." I swear it seemed that the judge held back a tear. I marveled at why everyone was so emotional about my quest. I felt that I maintained complete composure. "The books are closed, Michael," he continued. "All the records from your adoption are sealed. I'm very sorry. There's nothing I can do."

That was one of the biggest failures of my life. Before this encounter I had a clear vision of finding my birthmother on this very day. Now my dreams were disintegrating.

The judge reached for a piece of scrap paper. "Maybe this agency can help," he said while scrawling an address. "Contact these people. They may be able to help you." He handed the barely legible name and address to me. I glanced at it dizzily, stuffed the paper in my pocket and returned to New Albany.

I came home and explained to Mom that my trip was in vain. "See, Michael, we told you!" Mom spoke quickly and almost didn't let me finish my sentence. "They told us when we got you that the books are sealed. They cannot give out any information."

My soul was hollow as I shuffled to my bedroom, for I had returned empty handed. As I undressed, I found a now very crinkled paper that the judge had given me and tossed it beside my wind-up alarm clock. Then I dug deeper into my pockets and found a small box with crunched corners. The amulet. I removed it from its soft cotton bedding and momentarily observed its shiny gold reflection in the dim nightlight. I neatly returned it to a dark but safe corner of my dresser drawer and quickly went to sleep.

## 3. From Crayons to Confusion

The first negative encounter I remembered as a result of being adopted was when I was seven. A little girl who lived down the hill exclaimed in a hateful voice, "I know something you don't know...you're adopted!" Although that was a familiar word, I wasn't fond of the tone.

"So what?" I fired back.

"Your mom is not your real mother."

Lost for words, I scampered back up the hill to ask Mom what was so bad about being adopted. Noticing my confusion, she reassured me that adoption was not bad, but beautiful. She even gave me the correct comeback words to say if I was ever challenged with that question again.

The next day I saw the girl again. When she brought up the same subject, I had Mom's words memorized: "I might be adopted, but at least I was picked out special and your parents had to take what they could get!" The girl ran into her house crying. She never confronted me with that issue again.

In elementary school I was neither adopted or non-adopted, or black or white. Life was as pure and simple as drawing with color crayons on Manila paper. My favorite compositions included various flying machines that propelled red and yellow flames. Pastoral scenes were green for grass and hills, blue for the sky, and an occasional house, horse, or man which rested on the lower green level about one-quarter from the bottom.

Although I was not fortunate enough to have saved one of those masterpieces, I do believe my personal feelings were reflected in my human characters who usually smiled in their frozen crayon states. I always had graphite or paint imprinted on the inside heel of my left palm from smearing my artistic works with the very hand that created them.

Lunchtime and recess were the highlights of the day. Mom would neatly slice a sandwich into four bite-sized triangles with some cookies or potato sticks that I would carry in a brightly colored lunch pail featuring popular comic book heroes. The playground offered kickball, dodge ball, and interesting bugs to catch.

Mom picked me up after school promptly and waited in the parking lot with the other mothers. Standing alongside each other, I noticed the mothers appeared much younger than mine. One of them remarked as I came to the car, "What a fine boy you have, Mrs. Watson. Where does he get that lovely curly hair?"

Mom's face would beam upon hearing any compliment about her son. "He's our adopted angel. We got him when he was three days old," she would say.

Although it was obvious to Mom that I was certainly special, it was perplexing to me. Maybe *special* was a synonym for *rare*. In that case I would be like a precious diamond, something that everyone would admire.

### Dreaming in the Truck Bed

We had a small farm thirty miles away. Dad, Mom, and I would go there on a weekend getaway. I rode in the bed of our green Chevrolet truck. I looked forward to the Play-Doh fragrance of wild roses which grew alongside the dusty gravel roads. If I were lucky, I would find a swarm of zebra swallowtails, a scene never observed on Grantline Road. Sometimes there would be a dozen or more fluttering underneath the arms of a tree. Swinging my badminton racquet until my arms were sore, I once swatted one, then squished its eternal beauty between two pieces of glass. Exploring the countryside, I would hurl dried dirt clogs against the trees, exploding them into rusty brown smoke.

I feared the loathsome spiders. I would always shake with terror inside the tilted outhouse, wondering if a fanged creature would fall from the ceiling onto my back. The outhouse was also a favorite place for red wasps to build their nests. Going into the outhouse meant invading their privacy. I had to enter politely, shut the door ever so gently, do my business and leave.

I would sit on the hump above the back tires in the truck and the fresh country air would pound into my face and hair. Sometimes the aroma of cow manure or skunk spray would suddenly appear, and Mom would return a scrunched smile from the cab window. Then I would lie on my back and gaze into the sky. Eight cylinders would rumble close to my ears and road bumps would rattle me to and fro. When Dad made a right turn, the entire heavens shifted accordingly. Flocks of birds would make a sudden, yet choreographed about-face in the middle of the sky.

Reaching the expressway, my vision consisted only of fluffy clouds floating on a gentle blue background. I could tell Dad was driving fast from the engine's strained roar. No matter how fast the truck sped, the huge clouds remained motionless.

The combination of the motor's clamor and the boundless sky overhead was mesmerizing. After several minutes of looking into the heavens, my brain informed me that I was looking *down*! I would panic, wondering what would happen if the laws of gravity suddenly reversed. I could fall directly into the clouds! Although the thought was absurd, the feeling was real.

My anxiety would dwindle as an unexpected bump from a stray stone assured me that I was perfectly safe, lying in the cozy bed of the Chevrolet. I would relax again and imagine falling back in time when the universe was created -- when I was created. Then I would wonder about the little girl who said I was adopted. Did she know something that I didn't?

During those childhood voyages I could never seem to lie back and enjoy that higher level of awareness. And, as an only child, I did a lot of dreaming in the back of that truck. I never once realized that my imagination would someday dispatch me on a twenty-year journey to find my beginnings.

At night I slept in a small bed in the extra room. The ruffling oak leaves and the symphony of bullfrogs and crickets were never tranquil, but lonely. There wasn't the familiar swish of passing cars or the screaming of impatient fire engines like on Grantline Road. I had no brothers or sisters, and I was always aware of my solitude. I suppose one always fears what cannot be seen, and when the lights were turned off, I shielded myself with the covers to ward off any spiders with a sense of humor that might drop from the ceiling.

### First Love

In 1976 I turned eighteen. There was a clubhouse in the Knobs that was known for its Saturday night dances. That's where I met Angela. She was seventeen and had long, dark hair and shapely curves. At semi arms length, she was revolving to a slow song with another young man. When she dislodged from the boy, she accepted my offer to dance. Luna moths flittered by incandescent lamps as we strolled to the windless balcony. After a few opening lines, she said she lived on a farm down the road where her parents grew watermelons.

"What do *you* do, Michael?" she asked.

I was currently working part-time at a bakery. Friends always jested that I rolled in the dough. The owner had the prestigious title of *Cake Decorator.* I was the pan washer. Every day after school I would slave away by a monstrous dishwasher. The owner would swirl *Happy Birthdays* in an air-conditioned room while I was sweating beside a giant furnace-like droid. Another short, hunched man who obviously spent his entire life there would roll semi-truck loads of dirty bakery pans smudged with a gooey mixture of cherry jelly, dried chocolate, and sticky glaze. He rolled. I washed.

"I'm an executive bakery assistant," I finally said, hoping that she would respond positively.

"Are you Iranian?" she asked without pause. I felt her eyes settle on my Middle Eastern nose.

"No. Why?"

"Just wondered."

Then I explained, as convincingly as possible, that I was special because *no one* could figure out what I was. After more small talk, we made our first date.

Her house stood across a small ragged bridge. When I arrived, she was removing her trapped black cat from the ceiling of the porch. I offered assistance, and she asked me to catch the feline while she released it to the floor. The fat animal was making low, gurgling sounds that sounded like a cross between fear and irritation. I could see the white claws fully extended from each paw.

"Please don't miss my kitty when I drop him," she implored. On a first date I felt it was important to demonstrate heroism. It would be an honorable thing to do--to help this damsel in distress.

On the other hand, I beheld the peril that lingered overhead as I peered up at the razor sharp knives.

I saw the pleading look on Angela's face. "Fire away," I said, squinting my eyes with my arms over my head more for protection than anything else. The frightened cat plummeted towards me. It adhered itself to my head. With my eyes still closed, I grabbed the beast on both sides of its chest. Then the law of gravity took over. The animal dragged its claws from my scalp and slowly ripped me into slices as it descended to the ground with a moderate thump.

"You dropped my kitty," Angela said with disappointment in her voice as I stood bleeding to death.

"No. I caught him. He's just fine...landed on all fours," I responded, redeeming myself as best I could.

Although our youthful minds were usually light years apart, Angela seemed to be the first person who understood my desire to find my biological origins.

### ALMA

I found the wrinkled paper that Judge Jameson had given me on my first journey to Indianapolis. It read, *ALMA* and gave a New York address. The acronym stood for Adoptees Liberty Movement Association. The judge had told me that this organization was helpful for adoptees searching for their birthparents.

After making a letter inquiry, I received a form letter professing to put my name and birth date in its files for a small membership fee. If my birthmother would do the same, a *match* would occur.

Sending the money was like betting on a Kentucky Derby horse. What if my birthmother never filled out the same form? Did she have the money to send? Was she even still alive? Nevertheless, I eagerly filled out each blank I could answer.

Martha Velia Watson. Born March 15, 1920. Author's adoptive mother at eighteen years old.

Betty Stewart. Author's birthmother. Born June 29, 1935. Died September 19, 1981. Photo at age fourteen.

Betty (Stewart) Price and daughter, Debra Kay Price. Debra Kay was born December 6, 1955. Before her second birthday she mysteriously disappeared.

I had never heard of an organization that was on my side as an adoptee. It was certainly not a topic brought up during casual conversation with my adoptive parents. Actually, other than myself, I hardly knew anyone else who was adopted.

Above *Mother's first name* I wrote Betty. I was sure of that. For *Maiden name* I wrote Price, but wondered if that could have been her married name instead. Arriving at *Father's name*, I felt nauseous from my ignorance and curled a bold question mark.

After returning the form with a money order, I received a small booklet entitled, *Official ALMA Searcher's Guide for Adults.* The organization was founded three years earlier by Florence Fisher and offered mutual support for adoptees. The publication quickly confirmed that I was not the only adoptee concerned with his origination. A mosaic of smiling adoptees reunited with their biological relatives gleamed from the brochure, and I dreamily transported myself into the pictures.

Trudging through the booklet was painfully solitary, for I didn't feel there was an adult I could turn to for help. Nonetheless, after braving my way through the pages, I was confident that I would discover a way to contact my birthmother. She would probably be married, or remarried, and I imagined having sisters and brothers. She would be glad about finding me and knowing that I was all right. My mind, pondering the possibilities, happily branched into many tangents.

I waited and waited. Other than receiving a couple more newsletters about recent matches and reunions, nothing for me and nothing about my birthmother arrived.

## *4. Second Search*

In 1977 I turned nineteen. Mother's Day and my birthday were always times that triggered thoughts of my early existence. On Mother's Day I bought a nice card for Mom. Grantline United Methodist gave every mother a small pot of marigolds. But I also thought about my other Mom. After all, she was the one who gave me life. I could have been abandoned on someone's front porch, aborted, or tossed into a dumpster.

My birthday also reawakened the personal quest that slumbered in my soul. Surely that date evoked thoughts from my birthmother -- like those nine months, when I kicked violently in her womb during the last throes of pregnancy, ripping her insides out as I was born. Surely she remembered those agonizing pains of labor. There must have been times when she saw a boy resembling her and wondered, "Is he my son?" Maybe she had February 25 marked on her calendar, imagining my growing up one year at a time. She had to wonder what I looked liked, if I was all right, and what I was doing at the present.

The worn, wrinkled pages of the Bible crackled as Mom leafed back to the beginning of Matthew. Mom told me I was christened at two years of age. Ritually sprinkling a few drops of water onto my forehead, the minister paved my way into Christianity. The church congregation still affectionately remembered when I recited I Corinthians 13 from memory. Now I found myself rereading that holy book, not to refresh my memory, but to find an ancient, yet timeless truth buried in its words. I had always felt I was conceived from the powers of the universe. Maybe I too, like Jesus, was chosen to fulfill a divine mission.

I wondered what moral instruction I would have received from my birth family. A hallowed book from one family could be the other's Koran or a Sutra. My face did not resemble a typical American, so I could have been Jewish, Muslim, or Buddhist.

Even though I loved my adoptive parents, there were many times that I felt that I did not belong in the grand picture. Although I was free to do what I wanted, I also felt trapped in an impenetrable glass sphere. Up until this point, the sphere was my three-story house on Grantline Road.

Mom baked hot biscuits for dinner. Dad bickered about too much salt that mom sprinkled into the gravy she prepared from the drippings of fried bacon. I walked into the front yard, then down the hill to view my home from a broader perspective. The diary of my childhood unfolded as I peered into the sphere. I imagined dashing down the hill using Mom's green towel as a cape fluttering behind me. I always dreamed of flying. I remembered Mom holding a jar in one hand and a hole-punched lid in the other as I inserted lightning bugs. I visualized Aunt Arlie and Uncle Henry pulling down the driveway, coming all the way from Dayton.

I was filled with a sort of reverence. I was grateful to have two parents who cared for me, who *rescued* me from possible terrors of the past. Betty Price was the heroine who gave me the gift of life. My parents, on the other hand, were the heroes who *sustained* my life.

Although Mom still called me *special,* the word became like an old cliché. A former, positive preconception of the word was lost every time it was uttered. My father was unknown. Surely there was nothing *special* about being illegitimate. I agonized that I didn't know where I fit into this puzzle of life.

I was a bastard.

The joy I rendered to my adoptive parents must have been in direct proportion to the anguish and despair I brought to my birthmother. Did I enrich my adoptive parents lives through the deprivation of my birthmother? Was I the pivotal point between someone's happiness and another's suffering? Was there a void in my parents' lives and I was the cure? I was a gift to my parents, but at the same time I was the sacrifice of my birthmother. I did not feel special anymore, in any sense of the word.

Hallucinations of my birthmother haunted me. Was she a beautiful princess or a prostitute? Was I the product of rape? Incest? Was I conceived from sacred love or lust? Was I a survivor? And if so, what did I survive? Did my birthmother die? And if so, should I mourn at her grave? Was she an alcoholic or drug addict? If I unknowingly married a sibling, wouldn't that be called incest? Was relinquishing a child an ultimate act of a mother's courage or cowardice? My dreadful imagination never evaporated into spoken words but remained sluggish in my brain. I never expressed any such feelings to Mom, and Dad was not the right person for such discussion.

I remembered when my voice dropped an octave. The hair on my legs started to turn dark, and later on my arms. Black hairs sprang from my chest. I was transforming into a monster never seen by human eyes. I could not look to my father to determine my physical destiny. He was tall, with a smooth chest and had thin blond hairs on his limbs.

My other nightmare was losing my hair. Dad used to take me to Pope's Barber Shop as a child. One morning, as I was sitting bravely on the elevated swivel chair, old man Pope made a comment that I have not yet forgotten, "Boy, oh boy! Look at that thick, curly hair!" he exclaimed while snipping the back of my head. "I'll bet you'll go bald before you're thirty!"

Pope must have predicted an accurate forecast, I concluded, for he had barber tools and paraphernalia all over the small shop, including four taxidermed deer heads protecting each wall like ancient gargoyles. Since I was ten at the time, I calculated that my life would be over in just twenty more years.

I scheduled a second odyssey to Indianapolis. When I told Mom she hurled the same, "But they said they could not give you any information!" It was always difficult for me to accept no for an answer. I softened Mom's worries with a kiss yet repeated the journey.

This time I had a plan.

The huge parking lot of Community Hospital swallowed the Biscayne like a monster. The enormous building didn't look anything like the meek photo of the postcard Mom had given me years ago. I asked for the manager in the records division and told him my request.

"My name is Michael Price," I had changed my name. "I was born in this hospital on February 25, 1958. My mother's name was Betty Price. I need to see her medical records. She died, and I need to know if there are any hereditary illnesses that I should be aware of."

I was certain the word "adopted" was taboo at the hospital, and was careful not to utter it. However, I didn't fool the employees, who briefly looked up to see the poor soul searching for his mother and then returned their heads to their medical papers. They looked at each other shaking their heads.

"I'm sorry, sir. We cannot show you that information," the records manager said.

"I even know the doctor who delivered me...Dr. Fitzgerald. Surely you have records..."

"I'm sorry, sir." I seethed when everyone called me "sir" right before giving me a negative answer. "Medical records are personal and confidential."

"Look," I pleaded, this time raising my voice. "What if there is cancer or diabetes in her family? Don't I have a right to know that? I'm nineteen. I am an adult. I have a right to know where I came from!" Whoops. Unfortunately, my mouth was traveling at the same speed as my brain.

"We're very sorry," resounded the broken record. "We cannot release any data here."

Then, from out of nowhere, a subliminal message crept into my mind, perhaps from the pages of the *ALMA* workbook. "Can you please show me the written law that says I am not allowed to know information about my birthmother?"

Same answer.

I stormed down the long hall. Then I saw something by the information booth that brought me to a halt: a rack of postcards. This must have been where Mom bought the postcard when I was born, I thought. The pictures were different, however, and one card showed the same frontal view of the hospital, but it was shrouded on the edges by giant trees. The hospital appeared to be at least four times larger than it was depicted in 1958. I quickly observed that I was unnoticed and pocketed one for a souvenir.

Then I drove back to the county building, and the elevator lifted me again to the familiar floor. The judge was the same, but seemed to have less hair. I wasn't sure if he recognized me, but after I repeated my request from two years earlier, he returned with the same negative answer, this time with a more profound finality.

I went home. My plan had failed. There were records in those archaic edifices that were rich in detail about my birthmother-- about why she had to give me up, about who my father was, about my brothers and sisters. They knew who she was, but they would not tell me.

I arrived home a few minutes before midnight. Mom and Dad were still waiting up. I didn't feel like answering any questions so I went straight to bed.

# 5. Danger in the Snow

I was never a stranger to death. As a child I remembered many funerals I attended. I would stand beside Mom at the coffin and hear her remark how peaceful and nice they looked. One time she gave a quick kiss on the forehead of a corpse. Another time I forced myself to touch the hand of one of the doomed. It was cold and rigid.

The faces of the dead appeared before me. Although they were not genetically connected to me, I had nevertheless addressed them as aunt, uncle, grandpa, and grandma. I never physically resembled any one of them.

I believed in the Destiny of Things. If it were my turn to leave the earth, then that fate should not be questioned. I shouldn't have been afraid of such an insignificant thing as death. But I was.

Mom had just ripped away the month of January from the kitchen calendar. As intensely as spring reminded me of sprouting Easter tulips, the fragrance of Southern Indiana air and immortal youth, winter made me think of death. The cold wind and snow was not merciful to humans. The weather had become treacherous, and the news told everyone to stay off the roads except for dire emergencies. I could understand how residents could be awed by the uncontrollable beauty that blanketed the earth, but at the same time I was perplexed at how one could withstand several months of perilous cold while waiting for the warmth of spring.

It was Saturday, the day I always drove to Angela's house. Against my parent's wishes I left, wearing only a wind breaker and light gloves and kept warm mostly from the heater of a banana-colored Camaro Dad helped me buy. I drove carefully, for it had become almost impossible to go around a curve without sliding. I turned onto the country road that led to Angela's house.

Featheringill Road twisted like a writhing snake. About a mile from Angela's home, I descended what was to be my last hill. Driving no more than thirty miles per hour, I saw there was no more road in front of me, only a field of snow. As I applied easy pressure to my brake, the car slid into a silent oblivion of whiteness. I had driven into a four-foot drift. I tried to back up, but the Camaro's wheels spun hopelessly in reverse.

The arm of the gasoline gauge lay in that small red area just under the 'E'. I resolved to remain in the warm car while I organized my thoughts. I couldn't stay there forever, I calculated. Then I wondered what the reaction of an astronaut would be if he casually noticed that his oxygen tank said zero. I knew no one would detect my dangerous dilemma because no one would be as dauntless as I to travel on Featheringill's icy road. I blew warm air into my clenched gloves, turned off the engine, and set off on foot.

The wind pierced my windbreaker like shards of glass. Breathing made me dizzy and I covered my mouth and nose with my gloves. The snow was deep and I became tired after only a few steps. The wind rang through my ears, and I found it impossible to cover my nose, mouth, and ears at the same time. My right ear remained exposed.

In the blurry distance was an old house. I prayed that someone would be there. Trudging through the thick whiteness, the apparition became larger. My tennis shoes had become wet from the moist snow, and my feet began to burn. I couldn't feel my toes. I immediately remembered my Uncle Elmo who froze to death in the cow pasture. Dear God, I thought, I was going to meet the same doom as my father's brother.

Nearing the old house I discovered that it wasn't a house at all, but an abandoned shack. Breathing became increasingly difficult because the freezing air entered my lungs and made me cough. My ears and nose began to burn, and my balance was poor because I could not feel my feet. I fell twice. I turned back and could no longer see the yellow car. My mind raced. Something told me that going back would mean sure death, so I continued in the same direction, silently pleading that someone lived on that road.

I switched hands to relieve the burning of my right ear. I had to breathe, but the freezing air turned the wetness of my mucous membranes into instant ice. My mind was filled with horror thinking about the terrible death my uncle experienced.

I saw another house in the distance and forged blindly toward it. I started to cry. The wind showed no compassion and attacked the moistness of my eyeballs. When I came to the house, I knocked and a middle-aged lady answered.

"Mmnsd!" I garbled in one syllable. My mouth was frozen shut. There was no feeling in my lips. I rubbed my mouth to cause friction, like one who rushes to remove embarrassing spaghetti sauce on a first date. I imagined her thinking I escaped from a mental hospital.

"M-may I c-come n-nside?" My request was more understandable.

"Just a minute," she said. "Let me ask my husband."

Then she shut the door. I waited, still rubbing my lips in case I had to speak again. Each second went by painfully slow. One minute passed. Then two. I thought of the possibility of her not returning. I thought about Uncle Elmo. Maybe her husband told her to ignore me.  Maybe she really didn't have a husband and was frightened of me.  Maybe...

"All right.  Come in," the lady said standing at the halfway opened door.  I stumbled inside.

It took several minutes to feel normal again as I quivered above the heater vent.  I called Angela and her brother finally rescued me with his John Deere.

I stayed at Angela's house the next two nights until the wind ceased and the sun melted the ice from the back roads. Her parents obliged me with the guest room, complete with a crackling wood stove.  I stayed awake late both nights, giving silent thanks for being alive.

# 6. Third Search

D raped in black robes, the Class of '80 received their diplomas. I was 22. After four years, I had earned a degree in business. Mom gave me a kiss. Dad grumbled about me selling my guitar and finding a *real* job.

The summer months passed quickly. Then came the glory of autumn, a season one could actually smell in southern Indiana. Light rain dampened the already fallen leaves and the aroma rejuvenated the senses. The crisp air gently massaged one's face. The annual Harvest Homecoming commenced and the participants ranged from toddlers to the old timers who molded the charisma of New Albany.

Residents walked for blocks carrying folded lounge chairs, aligning themselves tightly along the street in preparation for the opening parade. Colorful floats, high school marching bands, and the Kiwanis mini-bike rodeo cavorted down the street. Clowns threw handfuls of bubble gum into the crowds and children scrambled for them. The following day would render food and game booths all the way up and down Pearl and Market Streets. Vendors would sell candied apples, cider and homemade chocolate fudge. The thick smoke from the Bar-B-Q chicken never bothered the glass blowers, who continued to spin delicate animal caricatures and merry-go-rounds.

Daughters looked like their moms. Sons resembled their fathers. I didn't look like anyone. My romance with Angela had sadly perished, and I felt alone amidst the thousands of spectators. I yearned for home, wherever that was.

On November 21, I dressed warmly, filled my gas tank, and returned to Indianapolis. I found North Delaware and parked where 2115 used to be. All the houses urgently needed a fresh coat of paint. The trees were gruesome without leaves.

I knocked on a familiar door. This time somebody was home. I introduced myself to an old lady, who promptly departed inside to get her husband. The couple must have felt my sincerity, for they escorted me inside to a dusty davenport patterned with large paisleys where I sat and sank halfway. The old man's forehead wrinkled, then he said he remembered a Betty Price that used to go bowling down the street every Wednesday night. He said that she walked with a limp, was short, and died in an auto accident many years ago. By the look on his face, I could tell he was struggling to assess his recollections. Somehow I resolved that he wasn't speaking about my birthmother. After a few moments the man started crying, and when I asked what was the matter he composed himself and told this story:

"I once had a good friend who was adopted," he began, wiping a tear with a faded handkerchief that he fetched from his front pocket. "He didn't know that fact until he was about your age, when he found the documents between the pages of the family's old Bible. He became furious at his parents for not telling him, packed his belongings, and vowed never to return. The biggest tragedy was when he found his real mother a few miles away."

"What happened?" I asked nervously.

"When she answered the door she said, 'I didn't want you when you were born,' his voice was broken and tears welled up in his eyes once again. '...and I don't want you now.'"

Jeez, I thought. Would I be strong enough to handle that ordeal? I felt sorry for the old man and his friend, but I couldn't relate that incident to me. How could a woman whom I had never met hurt me? I also remembered my childhood friends asking me if I hated my mother for giving me up for adoption. Likewise, I would think, how could I hate someone who was only a hazy apparition in my brain?

The man wiped his eyes, gave a grandfatherly smile and handed me an opened telephone directory. As I wearily gazed at the hundreds of Prices listed, I wished my last name had been *Zarnowski*.

I began to dial.

"Hello. My name is Michael Watson," I commenced. "The reason I am calling is because I was adopted here in Indianapolis, and I'm searching for my birthmother. Her name was Betty Price, and I was wondering if you have ever heard of her."

I received a different response every time. For the few numbers that didn't give busy signals or never picked up, most people were congenial. There were a couple of people who were pretty rude. One person thought I was a lunatic. Some would hang up on me. I always wondered if the latter knew the woman I was seeking or was the woman I was seeking but was frightened to say. I didn't know anything about selling in those days, but I realized afterwards that those seven straight hours constituted my first education in telemarketing.

I also didn't realize how hungry I had become until the elderly lady asked if I wanted something to eat. When I gave her a positive answer, she disappointed me with a plate of lemon cookies and a glass of milk. Nevertheless, I devoured every cookie without leaving a crumb and continued calling between swallows and gulps.

The sky turned to unpolished platinum gray. The telephone was an old rotary style and its cumbersome weight was cemented to the Queen Anne table. If a number had a zero in it, the dial would take forever to spin back to its original position. The dial was stiff and my fingers became sore. For two hours I had been calling with no luck. Then the man and his wife reappeared with interlocking hands and said, "Michael, we are going to watch TV at our friend's house in Beech Grove. We're gonna find out who shot J.R. You can stay here calling as long as you like. Just be sure to lock the door when you go back to New Albany."

I couldn't believe it. They were going to leave me there by myself. I was amazed how anyone would be that trustful of someone they had never met before. Then I remembered what they were talking about. That was the night the world would find out who shot J.R. Ewing on the *Dallas* episode. While over twenty million Americans would be glued to their television sets, I would be glued to a telephone, calling every Price in the Indianapolis phone book.

The couple left. I continued dialing. I became bored with my canned introduction and tired of all the rejections and snub remarks. My stomach growled for food again, but I didn't want to raid the couple's refrigerator. From my chair I could see the nightlight reflecting off yellow kitchen walls. Fantasizing about the delicious food hoarded somewhere in there, I began to salivate. The unwelcome illusion of lemon cookies entered my mind and made me sick. I needed *real food*. Taking two steps towards the kitchen I remembered the woman's words. "Keep on calling...lock the door." She did *not* give me the permission, however, to eat them out of house and home.

Marking my place in the phone book with a pencil I went outside, remembering to insert a thick piece of paper in the door jam so I wouldn't be locked out forever. I drove down North Delaware and found a fast food chicken place. I made a hefty order and retuned to the elderly couple's house with one hand on the steering wheel and the other in a bag of French fries. I accomplished a few more calls, dialing with a fresh finger. I smashed the empty chicken container in the trashcan, licked my greasy thumb and drove home. I left a nice thank-you note beside the telephone. This time I locked the door.

*"The surface of the Earth is the shore of the cosmic ocean...We have waded a little out to sea, enough to dampen our toes, or, at most wet our ankles. The water seems inviting. The ocean calls. Some part of our being knows this is from where we came."*
**Carl Sagan.**

# 7. In Search of Diamonds

In 1981, I began career hunting. A couple of weeks later a secretary from my college called, saying Shalaars Diamond Company needed a management trainee. I did need a steady income, and I was certainly not becoming rich from a guitar instruction course I had developed for aspiring musicians. I agreed to an interview.

I replaced the receiver and re-examined my talents: I failed miserably in accounting. I abhorred facts, figures, and wearing polyester suits. I wanted the autonomy of waking up when I wanted and writing memorable songs that would be hummed long after I was gone.

But I needed more money. I walked over and straightened my college diploma and blew off a layer of dust.

For my interview the following week I wore my blue suit, the only one I possessed, and added a red, white, and blue striped tie Dad had given me that clamped onto my shirt collar. My resume was skimpy from only working in a mom and pop bakery. I did work part-time at Zemartan's jewelry store when I was twenty. I failed to say, however, that my duties were sweeping the floor and delivering repairs in the run-down car of my boss.

The manager wore a drab brown suit with a stiff white collar that prevented him from turning his head very far. He directed his arms towards the jewelry showcases saying bluntly, "This is our product – fine jewelry and diamonds. We sell engagement and wedding rings. One of our salesmen quit and we need someone else. Does this sound like something you would like to do?"

"I..."

"Of course, we really don't know if you can sell, but we could give you a try. You will also need to spend some time on the phone touching base with our old customers."

"Yeah, I mean, Yes, Sir!" I said. After seven hours of calling every Price in the Indianapolis phone book, I felt I had a head start in the telemarketing department.

I was given a "pre-employment examination" during which I was asked a myriad of personal questions such as, 'Have you ever smoked marijuana? ...taken drugs? ...stolen anything?'

I felt a sudden weakness as adolescent memories flooded back. A hard pack of Marlboros used to bulge from my denim jacket that sported a sew-on patch of the never-victorious coyote from the *Roadrunner* cartoon. In those days, a brusque appearance seemed deviantly heroic, like the bad guys in comic strips whom one really wants to see prevail. I had developed acne and a low self-image. When I saw the proofs of my eighth grade photograph, I was so horrified that I demanded it not to be put into the yearbook. Instead of my picture, there were merely the words, "Sorry, no photo."

A trophy-like joint of marijuana nestled in my Marlboro box. One day, the principal came to my classroom and roared, "Watson, take me to your locker!"

I obeyed.

"Open your locker," he continued.

I made two nervous attempts at my combination dial. On the third try it opened.

"Remove your Marlboro pack," was his third order. My throat got dry.

"Open the cigarette box."

I did.

"Take out the joint."

I did that too, and for years afterwards I would kick myself for not shoving it down my throat to forever hide the evidence.

"Come with me to my office," was his final command. Then he called Mom.

That was the most terrifying day of my life. Mom preached a sermon that I heard from her several times afterwards, "Michael," she said, "How could you do that? Why do you think we took you to church all these years?" *We*, she had said. I don't remember *Dad* ever going to church. "Your life could be ruined because of this!" she continued deliriously.

Dad told me that I might have to go to a correctional institution. "They'll make you behave there," he exclaimed when he was drinking. He also told me a few times that they were going to give me back to the Indians. Being an adoptee, that pun was never funny.

"He's adopted. We got him when he was three days old," Mom said to the principal apologetically. "We've always taught him right from wrong. I don't know why he would do this." Although I was convinced that being adopted had no connection with my abnormal behavior, I didn't interfere with Mom's less-than-scientific inference.

I had sensed the end of my life. Although frightened to death, I felt more sorry for Mom than for me. She loved me so much. Now, here I was, busted for drugs at the tender age of fourteen.

"I was caught for having marijuana in junior high school." I humbly confessed to Shalaar's manager, straining not to lower my eyes in submission. "But I've never touched it since."

The manager gave a half smile and said, "When applicants say they have *never* touched pot, I figure they *must* be lying.

Honesty is held in utmost regard in this business, Mr. Watson. Please understand that we ask these personal questions because we want to make sure we hire trustworthy individuals."

I began to feel intimidated. The manager said that all employees were "highly encouraged" to take a polygraph. Then my mind flashed to the two blue vinyl chairs with aluminum legs that I had taken from my English class in college. I somehow wanted to give credence to my guitar instruction course and thought a modern touch would do the trick. It was the only thing I had ever remembered taking that did not belong to me. When I met Mom at the front door with the bulky fixtures, I crossed my only two available fingers behind my back and told her I bought them at a yard sale.

The jewelry career that I had yet to begin had already ended. What could I say I wondered? The needle would probably explode off the polygraph machine's printout if I told them I premeditated that heist for three months.

"So, what do you say, Mr. Watson? Do you think you can sell diamonds?"

This was the grand finale. I had never sold jewelry before. Neither had I sold cookies, used cars, or real estate. Then I worried about the blue chairs again. Getting the job was one anxiety, passing the polygraph was another. What would I say to the polygrapher?

"Yes, I know I will do a great job." I said with strained confidence.

My employment would commence on September 15, of course, as long as the polygraph results were okay. We exchanged a firm handshake, and I left. The polygraph was scheduled for the following week.

Returning home, Dad muttered that it was time I started looking for someplace else to live. I guess he was right. Some kids get evicted from their homes as soon as they finish high school. And many of those can't find jobs, get into trouble with the law, and beat up their wives, I continued to ponder. Mom said that I should continue to live at home and that I was not hurting anything.

I worried every day before the polygraph examination. I had been giving lessons on those blue chairs for the past two years. I visualized my polygraph appointment. "Yes, sir," I imagined saying. "I *did* steal two chairs from my university, but I promise I will never do that again."

My stomach twisted the day before the appointment. I could no longer bear the tension, so I crammed the chairs into the back of the old banana-colored Camaro and returned to the college. I hauled the chairs back to the English building and into the same vacant class I had seized them.

I cleared my conscience. My criminal record was now pristine. I had never stolen anything, I justified to myself. I merely *borrowed* those chairs for two years.

The next morning I went to the polygrapher. He was a small-framed man who appeared to be in his fifties. He wore a detective-type hat and had small, beady, red eyes. I remembered friends suggesting that I hire an investigator, like this man, to find my birthmother, but I always fervently refused.

"Here you go, Mr. Watson." he said, strapping the instruments to my chest and fingers. "I will ask you some normal questions to get started. There's no need to worry about anything. Just relax."

Right, relax. I wondered if *he* had ever been subjected to such a dehumanizing contraption. I had never seen a polygraph machine before, but its clumsy knobs and level indicators appeared more ancient than futuristic.

"Okay. We're ready!" His voice rose to an enthusiastic level. "Is your name Michael Watson?"

"What?"

"Just answer yes or no please."

"Y..yes."

The polygraph machine whirred, then I noticed it marking black zigzags on the paper that slowly poured from it. "Please look straight ahead at the wall, Mr. Watson,"

I obliged.

"Do you live on Grantline Road?"

"Yes."

"What is your mother's name?" He paced his questions slowly and deliberately.

"I have two mothers. One is named Martha Velia and the other is Betty Price." I said that in one breath, not realizing where the words came from.

"Excuse me, Mr. Watson?"

"I was adopted. My adoptive mother is Martha. I've never met my birthmother..."

"Okay." He sighed. "I can see you are a little nervous. Forget about that question. Let me ask you, have you consumed any illegal drugs within the past six months?"

In the past six months? I was getting ready to spill my guts that I was busted for *Panama Jack* at fourteen.

"No, sir," I answered.

He paused and made a few scratch marks on his clipboard. The polygraph machine continued to whir.

"Have you taken anything of value within the last six months?"

Then the postcard from Community Hospital somehow intruded into my mind! I suddenly wished there was a thumbtack in my shoe and I could pierce my toe and send the machine into a frenzy. "Yes!" I admitted. "I took a postcard from a hospital."

"A postcard?" The polygrapher shrugged.

"Yes. It was where I was born..."

"Mr. Watson, I am speaking about *anything of value*. I don't mean candy bars or paper clips that you might have taken as a child. Now, let's start over. Have you ever stolen *anything of value* within the last six months?"

Wait a minute, I thought. I had just caught on to this *six months* thing. Then I realized that I could have safely kept those chairs that I had returned the day before.

"The only thing I have ever taken is two chairs from my college but I returned them yesterday."

"When did you take these chairs?"

"Two years ago." The silence was disturbing. I could feel my heart in my chest.

"Two years ago? And you returned them yesterday?" Was that a question, I wondered? He rolled his eyes and continued. "Other than the two chairs that you took from your college, have you ever taken anything of value within the last six months?"

"No," I answered solidly.

I continued staring at the wall. The sound of the machine broke the silence.

"Okay, Mr. Michael. We're done."

"Do I get the job?" I asked.

"It is your employer's decision whether to hire you. We only give the data to them." He gave a half smile and ushered me out the door.

My palms were sweaty, one of the variables the polygraph machine measures. I was also positive that the darn gadget detected my throbbing heart. Anyway, I wiped the moisture on my pants and went home.

The musty downstairs apartment had been vacant for years, so I eventually claimed it as a place of quiet solitude. I had assembled a small music studio and was finishing the recording of a song. Dad appeared around the corner as the final chord resounded.

"What do you think of that one?" I asked with a smile while fading the volume slider.

"Crit, you know I don't understand all that racket. That's just a waste of time and money," he said, viewing the pulsating red lights from the console. I was never fond of my middle name. It came from my Grandpa Crit and I was told dad mumbled it in his sleep before I was born. Mom heard the commotion and scrawled the horrible word on a piece of paper. I realized at a young age that nice words don't begin with *cr: creep, crap, crud, crumb,* and *crotch.* The rhyming words seemed equally disgusting. *Spit, zit, sh...* "You're just one in a million, Mi-kel Crit. Don't you realize the percentage of people who succeed at that silly music racket?"

Very, very small, I thought humbly to myself. Dad was always street smart.

The next day the manager called, instructing me to start on Saturday. I arrived promptly with my blue suit, a professional smile, and my clamp-on tie. I was in the diamond business! My first duty was sweeping the floor. Besides being dressed more formally, the only difference in sweeping the floors at Shalaars was that I would be using a vacuum cleaner instead of a broom.

Someone had rested a styrofoam cup full of hot coffee on the edge of the sales counter. After making about six or seven revolutions with the vacuum, I somehow wrapped the electrical cord around the cup, and launched it into the air on the manager's light brown suit.

He said an expletive. Then he repeated it three more times. Pointing his finger at the table edge he snarled, "I don't want anyone to set their coffee here again!" I imagined the cursed table turning into smoke and disappearing into oblivion. At least I was off the hook and was careful with the final strokes of the vacuum cleaner.

Coming home, I unlatched the metal clamp of my tie and tossed it across my shoulder. As usual, the television volume was high and an irritating reporter blared the bad news of the day. Dad watched from his ringside seat as he cautiously poked Mom's dinner into his mouth. I hunted for leftovers on the old stove, sometimes finding a delicious cold leg of fried chicken, then escaped downstairs into my private world.

*"If you are a poet, you will see clearly that there is a cloud floating in this sheet of paper. Without a cloud, there will be no rain; without rain, the trees cannot grow, and without trees, we cannot make paper. The cloud is essential for the paper to exist. If the cloud is not here, the sheet of paper cannot be here either. As thin as this sheet of paper is, it contains everything in the universe in it."*

**The Heart of the Buddha's Teaching. Thich Nhat Hahn. Permission of Parallax Press, Berkeley, California.**

# 8. The Mountain to Paradise

L ike the upstairs attic of childhood, I used the downstairs for dreaming also. I thought about my past, my birthmother, and my origins. I never looked like anybody. I never felt connected to anybody. Yet, I never felt completely alone. Maybe that was because Mom told me God was always with me. I wondered what it would be like to know my birthmother, and to be able to see a reflection of myself. Where did I come from? Where am I going? What is my purpose?

I slumbered into a dream.

Upon becoming a legal driver at seventeen, I remember spending Friday nights with Tony Higgins, Greg Martin, and Jesse Jenkins circling Frisch's Big Boy, a now-extinct carhop on Spring Street. Although too shy to initiate a conversation with the girls, most of the cruisers demonstrated their manhood by revving up their engines, except my car, the blue Biscayne. It was basically a miniature tank and hardly voyaged over fifty miles per hour when the accelerator was pressed to the floor. After ordering a cola, we would pour half of it onto the ground and refill the cup with sloe gin.

On one murky night we headed for a terrain of hills overlooking Louisville. On the way, we came to a train crossing and Tommy shouted, "Ride the rails!" After realizing what he meant, I was caught up in the peer pressure of driving on the railroad tracks. With much coaxing, I turned the Biscayne parallel to the tracks

and hopped on. My four-wheeled vessel had become the Santa
Fe Chief. Passengers of on-looking autos had never seen
a blue train before. I sounded two long beep-beeep's and
flashed my headlights from bright to dim. The bumpy tracks
made Greg spill sloe gin between his legs. Jesse waved at
spectators from the back.

We left the tracks and continued up the snaky hill.
Tony Higgins babbled about the girl that dumped him. Jesse
threw up out the window. The thick fog began to blind us.

"Your nose is bigger than your Dad's," Greg jested to
Tony before I made an unexpected sharp turn.

"Get out of here, man!" Tony fired back after we
straightened our slanted positions. "At least my dad didn't
give me a big strawberry nose like yours!"

"And where did you get that wild, kinky stuff on your head,
Watson?" Jesse groaned from the back as the Biscayne descended
steeply. "Oops. Forgot you're adopted."

"Look out!" Tony screamed. I squinted my eyes and slammed
my brakes. My vision was blurred. I didn't see that the road had
suddenly made a right angle turn. We were heading over the cliff.

The sound of tires sliding from the misty pavement onto
the wet soil was terrifying. A second later we hit a boulder. We
swayed out of the car and peered into the destiny that the boulder
denied us. The ravine sank into oblivion. Occupants of a nearby
house must have heard the impact, for we could see the graduating
silhouettes of a family behind their living room curtains, straining
for a glimpse of the tragedy. The Biscayne suffered only the loss
of a halogen eye. Tony, Greg, Jesse, and I survived.

I continued to dream.

One autumn, Tony Higgins's family moved southwest to
Hopkinsville, Kentucky. I drove down to stay overnight. The

next morning Tony took his cousin Steve and me to Pilot Rock, a mountain site that was renowned in his new homeland.

Arriving early, we jumped out of the car and raced to the top. Primitive steppingstones were awkwardly arranged, making us appear like galloping ostriches. Suddenly the bright sun disappeared as we spiraled up the huge cliff, as the steps led us to the mountain's center before it carried us upward. I was never much of an outdoorsman and never enjoyed mosquitoes, sharp thorny plants, or fat bees that buzzed at low frequencies. Tony and Steve didn't complain so I stayed close behind them.

At the summit we were embraced by a bright yellow light. An endless ocean of autumn-colored trees blanketed the earth warmly. For the first time I grasped the magnificent size of the world. Although a complete circle revealed endless miles, I knew the view was such a small fraction of our planet. The air was chilly, I had forgotten to bring my coat, and there was deafening silence.

A seven-story fire tower stood at the mountain's top. With fearless hearts and careful footing, we climbed into the sky. The air blew cooler on my arms and face. Fighting gravity, we dared not look down until we reached the highest point of the tower. Viewing the earth from this elevation was a spiritual awakening--a complete freeing of one's soul. Tony flapped his arms and pretended to fly. The glorious view of Earth stopped my breath. I could see a longer radius of orange citrine miles as I turned in a circle. I peered downwards. The trees were tiny but seemed never-ending.

The numbness of the breeze stilled my thoughts. What if I were a victim of Pilot Rock? Surely some mischievous youngster had fallen from the tower. I could not escape the dreadful feeling that a misplaced foot would trip me to the land of the non-living. I clutched the side beams with white knuckles as I stared down. I imagined losing my grip, slipping, then falling to the tower's base. I envisioned grasping at air, for there was nothing to hold on to once I let go. The free fall would last mere seconds, and the scrapbook of my life would be played--at lightning speed. I glanced over to Tony and Steve. The wind was peacefully blowing in their faces while they continued to absorb the panorama. They both wore pleasant smiles.

Leaning snugly against a tower brace, I tightly covered my ears with my hands and closed my eyes. I prevented any wind from seeping through my fingers so I could not hear anything except an ocean-like roar, like the muffled rumble one hears when pressing a large seashell against an ear.

This must be death, I thought. I removed my hands and again gazed into an artist's palette of never ending trees. The universe resounded with a beautiful symphony that only I could hear. Although I was humbled to a single cell, I was also a living masterpiece with every physical organ working together like a perfect machine. Was I formed by the hands of a creator? Was I a wonderful offspring of the Earth? I realized the inextricable connection among the mountain below me, a lone tree in the distance, the sun that warmed my cheeks, and my mind to be able to discern the differences. One thing could not exist without the others.

In the evening I numbly drove back to New Albany. For the first time, I did not feel estranged from the cosmos, but merely a part of it. I couldn't grasp who or what was responsible for the paradise I beheld. Was the origin of this power inside or outside of me? I realized that although we are born from the creature we call woman, it is our universe that is our primal mother. The universe gave birth to our wonderful earth. The earth gave birth to me.

For once I realized that I am the sum total of all things. If I had fallen from the tower of Pilot Rock, my death would not upset the beautiful balance of the universe in the slightest, and it would be impossible for me to die without knowing my true creator.

1961.  Betty Price and children, Susie and Michael David.

Author's sister, Susie.

Junior High photos of author and sister, Susie, twenty years before either knew of the other's existence. The siblings met for the first time on July 5, 1996.

*Mufasa: Everything you see exists together, in a delicate balance. As king, you need to understand that balance, and respect all the creatures-- from the crawling ant to the leaping antelope.*

*Simba: But, Dad, don't we eat the antelope?*

*Mufasa: Yes, Simba, but let me explain. When we die, our bodies become the grass. And the antelope eat the grass. And so we are all connected in the great Circle of Life.*

**The Lion King. Disney Enterprises.**

# 9. Mother's Day

It was 1983, and Mom brought back a small pot of marigolds from Grantline United Methodist. I gave her a gigantic card crayoned with twelve red roses. To Mom, it was my thought and efforts that were priceless to her. I don't remember her ever yearning for material things. She squeezed me with both arms before I retreated downstairs.

I lifted my acoustic guitar from its stand and dragged my fingers across the strings. Mother's Day was always a joyous occasion for Mom and me, but at the same time it would submerge me into deep wonder. Maybe Mother's Day should be doubly joyous for I had two Moms! One who raised me from birth and the other one whom I hadn't met...yet.

Mom and Dad had told me about Dr. Fitzgerald and Raymond Demaree. They were the key characters of my adoption. Mom had said that Mr. Demaree was a "very old man" when I was born. I was now twenty-five. He was either unthinkably old or dead. I assumed the latter.

Returning my instrument to its resting place, I phoned Indianapolis information for a listing of Fitzgerald M.D., William. I couldn't believe I had waited so long to take on such an effortless but obvious endeavor. The operator answered immediately with the number, as if she were awaiting my call.

"Hello?" an older woman's voice answered.

"Hello, Mrs. Fitzgerald?"

"Yes?"

I realized I was listening to the voice of a woman whose husband delivered me. It was the closest connection I had ever made.

"My name is Michael Watson. Is Dr. Fitzgerald there?"

"Who is this?" she answered skeptically.

"Your husband delivered me in 1958. I was adopted then, and I am searching for my birthmother."

That last statement did not bring joy to the old lady, for she said that her husband had died several years ago.

"I'm sorry to hear that. Are there any records left?" I grasped, not taking a breath in between sentences. "Is there any information about my birthmother?"

"There are no more records. I'm very sorry," she responded humbly.

"But what about the hospital. Don't they have records?" I asked involuntarily, already knowing that answer.

"I'm sorry. There are no more records, but good luck to you." Then she hung up before I could think of another question.

Later that day I surfaced upstairs to tell Mom about that phone call. She looked at me with the familiar face that was a cross between wonder and disappointment. "Michael," she paused, "are you still looking for your birthmother?"

"Sure, Mom. You know I love you, but sometimes I have a little empty feeling."

"What would you ever do if you found her? Would you want to go live with her?"

"Of course not," I said emphatically. "I want to know who she is, that's all. I have the right to know where I came from. I want to know..." I searched for words, "what is my ethnicity."

"Michael, what if you find her? What are you going to do then? Maybe she has had a hard life. What if she would want you to take care of her? Maybe she doesn't have much money and would want you to support her." She continued to ramble. "Michael, I lived in fear for several years thinking that one of these days your birthmother would find you and ask for you back. You can't *realize* what I felt." She started to cry.

"What do you mean, Mom?"

"Michael, don't you understand that a social worker could have taken you away from us? Every time I heard a knock on the front door I thought it was either your birthmother or a social worker."

"Mom, please!" I wished I had kept my mouth shut. We had had this dialogue many times before. I realized that I could never have the same feelings as an adoptive parent. But on the other hand, I don't think my Mom could ever understand my feelings. In fact, sometimes it was hard for me to define why I hungered relentlessly to search for the unknown.

"Michael, just remember that I am your mother." Her tears receded, and she spoke with a solid boldness I had never heard before. "I don't want you to ever forget that. Do you understand?"

I could never bear to see Mom cry, but that was a moment I could not manage to give her an assuring hug. I came to the appalling realization that this whole adoption game had become a tournament between me and Mom.

*"Miss Sullivan had taught me to find beauty in the fragrant woods, in every blade of grass, and in the curves of my baby sisters hand.... I feel that her being is inseparable from my own, and that the footsteps of my life are in hers. All the best of me belongs to her-there is not a talent, or an inspiration or a joy in me that has not awakened by her loving touch."*

**Helen Keller. *The Story of My Life.***

## 10. Behind the Curtain of Fear

I have fond memories of Shalaars. Sheila Carr would toss grapes and cheese balls into my mouth from across the room while the manager was out. Roger would stalk the front door for an approaching jewelry prospect, extinguishing his cigarette into the ashtray as soon as the door opened, and making a quick swish through the air to dissolve the floating smoke. And I accidentally caught my tie inside a jewelry showcase while bending over and locking the door. When I rose up, the tie locked me into a hunched position. Then it came off! Everyone was shocked in amazement. Then they laughed hysterically. Apparently they had never seen a clamp-on tie before. It looked like one of my limbs had been detached like the cartoon depictions of a leprosy victim.

Resuming an upright position, I confessed that I didn't know how to tie a tie. The next day I bought several regular ties and commenced the laborious learning process of knotting a double Windsor. Even afterwards, the employees would lift my collar just to make sure I wasn't wearing a phony. The consensus was everything in the store must be real: no imitation diamonds, no artificial plants, and no fake ties.

Although I enjoyed working at Shalaars, slow periods would send me on a voyage of introspection. On many occasions I visualized Dad showing me his worn, wrinkled hands saying, "You see these, Crit? They have worked hard all their life." I was grateful to have such a job where I didn't have to exert so much physical labor and lift heavy pipes like him. Mom said that was the reason they sent me to college. Here I was, wearing a suit and a crisp white shirt, and all I was lifting were polished diamonds. I sometimes felt guilty, knowing my parents had sacrificed much of their savings for my education.

During a playful moment, Sheila asked my nationality. I smiled and answered stupidly, "I don't know. I'm adopted." She then asked if I ever wondered who my birthmother was. My smile turned more serious and I answered affirmatively. I also told her all the sketchy information I knew about my human beginnings.

"Then go find her!" she said demandingly.

I couldn't manage to reach her level of inspiration. "I already made many trips to Indianapolis," I replied. "They said the books are sealed. It's the law."

I went home very somber. I knew I was denied a very fundamental human gift: my ancestry. I pulled out the family photo album from the living room desk and flipped its pages. The first photo showed Mom holding me on her lap. The unmistakable signs of a proud mother shone from her face. Another picture showed Dad wrestling with me on the couch. He wore a bright smile that I had never before recalled. Then came my birthday scenes: one year old, two years old, three years old. At five, I was smiling behind my birthday cake while Dad helped me hold up five fingers. On the next page I was blowing out six candles. The next showed seven plastic horses parading around another cake.

Then I returned to the first page. My hair was dark and curly. The eyes were dark and huge. I compared my photos to my parents on the same page. Mom was plump and fair skinned with a roundish face. Dad was slim and lanky with light hair. What happened before page one, I asked myself? Was I even *born*?

I surely didn't resemble my parents. I have never resembled anyone on this planet, I reminded myself again. I quickly deduced that my birthmother was presently forty-five years old. I also knew that was a young age for a woman and that she would certainly be alive. I remembered when my adoptive mother was the same age many years ago. She was very attractive. I imagined my birthmother was equally beautiful.

Sheila Carr had reignited the embers in my soul to search for the past. Noticing my schedule read "off" for the next two days, I planned a final triumphant journey to Indianapolis. This time I didn't tell my parents. Every time I mentioned my search it caused pain and disappointment for them.

Friday's sun was scorching and the Camaro didn't have air conditioning. I arrived at the county building in the afternoon. Getting out of the car, I noticed my clothes sticking to my flesh from the suffocating humidity. The weather of Indianapolis seemed as unpredictable as New Albany: freezing one day and scalding the next.

I returned to the probate court, which was the only institution I felt had any record of my early existence. While the ancient elevator creaked upward, I wondered if Judge Jameson would recognize me. Would he bellow a fat "no" before I even said hello? Would he even be there? Would I have to start all over again with my interrogation? I mentally planned my request as I concentrated on the lighted floor numbers. The other passengers stared at their feet.

"Your Honor," I began after entering his chamber, "My name is Michael Watson. I was adopted on February 25, 1958. I have no history, no heritage, and no origin. Please let me know who my birthmother was."

I stood straight, paced my words evenly, and kept eye contact. I then realized that I wasn't interrogating but rather begging. As the judge gazed with concrete eyes, an awful silence followed. His appearance had not changed over the last eight years. I wondered if he recognized me, thinking "There is that darn kid again."

"Sit down, please," the voice said. I obeyed. The judge gave a long and penetrating stare, as if to ascertain my sincerity. He pressed a button on his desk, then spoke toward a small speaker, "Mrs. Green, please pull the court summary adoption record for Michael Watson, born 2-25-58. Make a copy and bring it to me."

A woman scuffled into the room with a sheet of paper dangling from her fingers. He took it and leaned way back into his mushy chair.

Devastating silence resounded once more. The judge remained expressionless as he scanned the document. The quietness was almost unbearable, and my mind created an artificial hum, like the wind on the peak of Pilot Rock. I was consumed with a blend of aspiration and terror. The judge was holding the secrets of my personal universe in his hands. Where did I come from? Why did my mother relinquish me? Who was my birthmother? I felt transported to the top of the fire tower, standing on that final edge.

Then he handed the papers to me.

"Here you are, Mr. Watson."

Fear embraced me with a tighter grip. Did I really have a right to see this information? I didn't know whether to look or not. Would I turn into a pillar of salt? Shouldn't I feel guilty for pursuing this? My adoptive parents are the only parents I've ever had. If it wasn't for them, I might not even be living.

I waited for the horror. I would now lift the veil imprisoning the dark forces of the past. The secrets of the unknown would finally be revealed as I drew *the Curtain* aside.

I reached for the paper and devoured the words faster than I could understand them. I feared the possibility of the judge snatching the paper from my hands and saying, "That's enough, Mr. Watson. You can come back again in ten more years."

But he didn't.

I relaxed, and reread the words from the beginning. It said:

June 16, 1958

Marion County Department of Welfare

Caseworker:  Mrs. Mildred Hardesty

| | |
|---|---|
| Name of Child: | Michael Crit Price |
| Date of Birth: | February 25, 1958 |
| Status: | Illegitimate |
| Brothers/sisters: | 1 half-brother |
| Color: | White |

BY WHOM PLACED:

The child was placed by mother's physician (unnamed), the attorney, Raymond Demaree, taking care of legal details, including an order from Probate Court to remove the baby from the hospital.

FATHER OF CHILD:

No information was secured.

MOTHER OF CHILD:

Mrs. Betty Price was interviewed in the office, following arrangements made by her attorney.  She came from Plymouth, Indiana, her home and will return there, she said, by the next bus.

Mrs. Price was a small woman, wore her hair in a pigtail. She also wore cheap jewelry and stale perfume. She said she knew nothing about the father of this baby. Some mutual friends had introduced them, and the child was conceived after they had too much to drink. She never saw her baby, and it was all like a bad dream.

She grew up with her parents. They were good people. When she was in the sophomore year, she quit school to be married. She was only 16 years old. She married Floyd Price, December 29, 1951. He was 26 years old. A child was born to them in 1953, named Michael David Price. On September 15, 1955, she divorced Mr. Price. She said he was never true to her.

She wanted nothing to happen to her first child, and that is why she would give us no more information about him or her family. She did say her parents lived near Noblesville, Indiana.

It was felt that Mrs. Price was not telling the truth and that she had been told what to tell our agency.

SIBLINGS:

There is one half sibling, Michael David Price. Nothing is known about him, except he is living with his maternal grandparents.

My energy drained. I didn't understand the words, people and places. "What does this mean?" I asked the judge brainlessly.

"Well, for one thing, it looks like you have a half-brother... Michael David."

"You mean that wasn't me?"

"No, you are this person," pointing to Michael Crit Price.

"I have a brother?" I repeated.

"Yes, and his name happens to be Michael, also. He would be...five years older than you."

"What should I do now?" The judge seemed to take on the mythical configuration of the birthfather I never knew.

"Well, it says here your mother's parents lived near Noblesville. Noblesville is just a few miles up the road past Carmel. Her parents could still be living there. Your mother never gave her maiden name. You might go to the courthouse there and see if you can find a copy of her marriage license to Floyd Price. Then you will be able to find out who your grandparents are."

His words cut with the precision of a diamond's edge. When I shook hands with the judge my energy level multiplied to that of a comic book superhero. I returned to the Biscayne where the interior was now blistering hot. I rolled down the windows and tried to keep cool from the onrushing wind as I sped to Noblesville.

I became oblivious of everything surrounding me. My eyes hardly veered off the long road even as I overtook the slower moving automobiles. After passing the town of Carmel, I darted into the Noblesville exit, instinctively finding the old courthouse and raced inside.

"Hello," I said, directing my words at the first person I saw. "Can you please find me the records of Betty Pri... uh, Betty *Somebody* who married a Floyd Price around..." I searched the court summary, "... December 29, 1951?"

"Mister, we are closing now," came a woman's voice from my right. Closing? I looked at my watch. It was three minutes before four in the afternoon. Another lady saw my urgency and started to dig into the files.

"Please hurry, Ma'am," I said involuntarily.

"I'm going just as fast as I can, Sir."

The other employees watched in confusion.

"I found my mother," I announced to everyone with radiance. "I was adopted. I have never known my birthmother until now. I'm going to find her today."

Two elderly ladies behind the counter smiled at each other. "How wonderful," I heard one say. "He was adopted. Isn't that precious?"

The lady who was digging returned. "I'm sorry sir. There's no information here. All I need are the names. Can you repeat those one more time?"

"Floyd Price is the man. I don't know Betty's maiden name."

"That's exactly what I checked, sir. There's no such..."

"Check some more!" I blurted. "I mean, there must be some record in there," my voice dropped to a more professional level.

The lady returned to the files hesitantly and shuffled again.

I yelled across the counter. "I have the date. December twenty...."

"We don't need the date," she interrupted. "I checked every Price that was married in Hamilton County. There is no one that matches that name."

The ladies' smiles faded into expressions of concern. The file lady turned to them and shook her head apologetically.

I started to feel sick. I wearily glanced at the court summary, then handed it to the lady. They all joined together in reviewing the people and places and told me there was nothing more they could do.

I stepped outside into the windless humidity and inspected the surroundings. Noble Nowheres-ville, I mused sarcastically. Then I began a brisk walk and increased my gait with every step.

My underarms and insides of my thighs were soaked from perspiration. I needed fresh clothes. There was a laundromat down the street and I aimlessly headed in that direction before I realized that I would have to sit naked while waiting for my clothes to wash and dry. I went to a drug store two doors down and purchased some deodorant, a toothbrush and small tube of toothpaste. Then I walked across the street to a discount clothing store and purchased a pair of pants and a shirt. I changed in my car in front of the courthouse. The hot seat scalded my legs.

I studied the court summary. 'It was felt that Mrs. Price was not telling the truth...' The words haunted me. But the facts were so specific! If a twenty-two year old woman would lie, then she wouldn't have given such detailed information. She refused to give her parents' names. That was all right. It would make my search a little more interesting. I continued reading.

'When she was in her sophomore year, she quit school to be married.' She obviously went to Noblesville High School. I walked around the corner to the town library in my new bright red sleeveless shirt and stiff blue jeans...shorts weren't in style. I blindly riffled through the high school yearbooks from 1952, the year she would have been a sophomore. I didn't know her last name so I just looked for every Betty, Betricia, etc. I could find. There were none. Then I found myself scanning for my own reflection. Most everyone seemed very average and American looking. The young boys had their hair slicked back strangely and the girls had weird hairdos.

Flipping the pages, I remembered not allowing my own junior picture to be published. What if she had the same low self-image as I did during those years of tribulation that many adolescents suffer? Should I have been looking for a, 'Sorry, No Photo?' I looked in the years preceding and succeeding. No luck. The court summary was becoming damp from my sweaty hands so I made a copy before it disintegrated.

With my elbows on the desk, I relaxed my chin in the cup of my folded hands as the sun turned red and poured a horizontal beam of light above my desk. The library was closing in forty-five minutes. Then I thought: 'She married Floyd Price, December 29, 1951.' Maybe there was an announcement in the local newspaper. If I found that, then it would also give her parents' names. The reference clerk handed me a microfilm of the Noblesville Topics newspaper for two weeks up until the date of my birthmother's marriage. I scanned the film unsuccessfully until the library closed.

Then I re-read that horrible sentence: "She also wore cheap jewelry and stale perfume." What is the definition of *cheap*? How can one tell at a distance if personal adornments are gold-plated or solid eighteen karat? Was she dripping in gleaming rhinestones or did she flaunt an ensemble of multi-colored plastic bangle bracelets? And what was the importance of that being documented? And what is *stale* perfume? Does that mean *cheap* also? And if so, are interviewers qualified to conclude the quality of fragrances? Did stale mean musty, sour, or decayed? I tried to erase the derogatory comments from my brain. She was my *birthmother*.

Most of the local businesses had shut down for the evening and the residents seemed to evacuate back to their homes. I roamed the town by foot until the sky turned opal gray and paused by a nearby phone booth. Since I still lived at home, I knew Mom would be deliriously worried by now.

"Hi, Mom."

"My God, Michael, where are you?"

"In Noblesville. It's about fifteen miles north of Indianapolis. Mom, guess what?"

"What?"

"I have a brother!"

"Michael, I know you like to kid your poor old mom. Where are you?"

"I went to Indianapolis again. The judge gave me a copy of the court summary of my adoption. I'm getting close to finding my birthmother. I'll be home tomorrow. Don't worry about me. I love you."

"Michael! Don't hang up! Wha..."

"Mom, my brother's name is Michael, the same as mine! I love you more than anything, Mom, but this is something I need to do. I hope you understand."

"MICHAE..."

"Good-bye." And I hung up.

Digging deep into my pockets, I could only exhume a few dollars and some change. I looked for a cheap place to sleep and ended up at the White Horse Inn. The room was small, the floors buckled, and there was no phone. The bed was framed with dark, thick wood, and ancient wrought iron fashioned jagged curls in the headboard. The sheets were folded down white and crisp. I lifted the pillow and buried my face into it. It smelled fresh.

I removed my clothes and twisted the single faucet knob on the shower. The coldness of the water momentarily revived my senses but did not ease my exhaustion. Nevertheless, I felt clean. I crawled into the bed, and the weight of my body sank into the abyss of the soft mattress. I felt my bones melt. The bed and I became one. I looked up at the ceiling. Then down to the floor. To my left. Then to my right. No spiders. I clicked off the light.

I awoke to a thin, bright stream of Saturday sunshine that found its way from the small opening of the curtains into my eyes. I was on a secret mission, a crusade to find the mystery woman, and now also my brother! I checked out early to explore the town.

I leaped into the Camaro, now rusting from the salt that is splayed onto Indiana's winter roads, and cranked down the windows. The morning air was cool and damp. This is where my birthmother was from. Maybe this is where I was conceived, where the egg and sperm united to create this body in which I now dwell. Maybe it was a one-night stand at the White Horse Inn. Anything was possible.

I came to a small church, parked my car, and entered. I heard singing from a distant room. Although I didn't see anyone, it sounded like the voices of six or seven adults trying to learn a hymn for the first time. I tiptoed my way to what looked like a tiny office. I found what I was looking for: a telephone and a fresh directory of Noblesville and surrounding towns.

Sitting at the small desk I discovered only twenty Prices listed. The phone was a rotary style and evoked memories of the old phone in the elderly folks' house in Indianapolis. I glanced around the room and saw a handsome depiction of Jesus on a wall. I closed my eyes, trying to drown out the off notes from the choir. Before I began the first number, I had my finger in the phone hole with the letter "M". Then for good luck I continued to dial "O" and then "M" again to spell the code word of my mission. I also realized that I had just dialed "666," and my aspirations slightly dwindled. Nevertheless, I inhaled deeply and proceeded with the process of elimination.

"Hello, my name is Michael Watson," I commenced to the first number. "I am adopted. The reason I am calling is because I am searching for my birthmother. Her name became Betty Price after she married Floyd Price. I also have a half-brother named Michael David Price. Do any of those names sound familiar to you?"

Although my script got better with each call, every person gave me a negative response. My leads were finished.

I solemnly drove to Noblesville High School. I parked in front, turned off the motor, and mostly just stared into the empty windows. I waited to feel a cosmic connection to the small town. Traveling thoughts entered my mind as I gazed. 'She quit school at 16... was a sophomore.' Why did she quit school so early? She didn't get pregnant with Michael David until three years later. Then I thought, I was not the firstborn. Why did she decide to keep Michael David, yet give me away?

I drove around haphazardly the rest of the day. A few pedestrians scampered around here and there. I realized that this excursion had come to an end. Sunday was a busy day at Shalaars. I had to get back home.

The courthouse was closed, so I tacked a copy of the adoption summary on the front door with my phone number at the bottom. I had also taken a black marker and inked through, "too much to drink", "cheap jewelry," and "stale perfume." Nobody's business.

I pulled into our driveway around seven in the evening. Peeking through the living room curtains was Mom's silhouette. I opened the familiar wooden door.

"Hello, everyone!" I greeted.

"So, you went back to Indianapolis. Well, what did you find out?" Mom asked with worry and anticipation. Dad lowered his newspaper just below his eyes to hear my answer.

"Here you are." I handed the court summary to them.

"What's this?" Mom asked.

"The judge gave it to me, Mom. This is the story of my life."

"How did you get this? I thought they said the records were sealed." Mom said.

"Never take 'no' for an answer, Mom."

We took turns reading the summary.

"So Price was her *married* name," Mom continued.

"Looks like you got a half-brother, Crit." Dad smiled. I was proud to share this new information with my parents and that I was tenacious enough to get it. I heard Dad keep repeating, "PLYmouth, PLYmouth Indiana," accenting the first syllable strongly.

We reread the summary together: "She came from Plymouth, Indiana, her home and will return there, she said, by the next bus." After locating a map, we saw the city was almost at the northern tip of the state. "That's right, Dad," I said. "But her parents were from Noblesville. I would be on a wild goose chase if I went to Plymouth, not knowing her maiden name."

Then before we retired for bed Mom said, "Me and your daddy are really happy for you, Michael. Don't you feel better knowing that your search is finally over?"

"What do you mean, Mom?" I asked.

"Well, you got the information you wanted, didn't you? You know where your birthmother came from and the circumstances. When she gave birth to you she had been divorced from Floyd Price. Back then people didn't have very much money. She probably couldn't afford to keep you."

"But, Mom, I haven't found her yet," I argued. "I just want to meet her at least one time. Don't you understand?"

"Michael, didn't you read what it said at the bottom?" Her finger went precisely to the beginning of the sentence. "It says right here that she probably lied about the whole thing. You could be searching for the rest of your life for nothing. You could be spending money on top of money. Then if you did find her, she could be an alcoholic, with no money, and then you would feel obligated to support her."

"Mom, for Pete's sake!"

"I'm just telling you the truth. I don't want you to be hurt. You should thank God that you have parents who love you very much. Do you realize that we couldn't love you any more than your friends' natural parents?"

The pride of my two-day achievement gradually resolved into shame.

"And I hope you don't think about driving clear to Plymouth," she continued. "We worried enough about you for the past two days."

"But Mom..."

"Michael, if and when you find your birthmother, I am behind you all the way. Just don't ever forget that me and your daddy are your *real* parents. What if your birthmother couldn't afford to put braces on your feet when you were a baby? You would be walking like the poor old man I saw at the store today. You should have seen him, Michael, the poor guy. One foot went straight out to the left, and the other went straight out to the right."

When I was two, a doctor had prescribed foot braces when Mom noticed my feet turned outwards. My feet were thus confined in an awkward metal contraption for the next two and a half years, forcing them into a "pigeon-toe" position. When I crawled, she always knew where I was from the clunking sound.

This time Mom did not get upset or cry. Her words were straightforward and had a sense of finality.

"PLYmouth. PLYmouth." Dad read the summary over and over until late in the night.

"If you have experienced hunger, you know that having food is a miracle. If you have suffered from the cold, you know the preciousness of warmth. When you have suffered you know how to appreciate the elements of paradise that are present. If you dwell only in your suffering, you will miss paradise. Don't ignore your suffering, but don't forget to enjoy the wonders of life."

**The Heart of the Buddha's Teaching.** **Thich Nhat Hahn.** **Permission of Parallax Press, Berkeley, California.**

## 11. Looking for Mother - Please Call

I strolled into work proudly the next day. "Well, guys, my birthmother was short, beautiful, and wore her hair in a pigtail!," I beamed.

"You found her?" Sheila Carr cheered.

"Not exactly. But ..."

My adventure was the talk of the day. The employees and manager took turns reading the court summary. They bombarded me with questions like, "Why don't you try this?"..."Why don't you try that?"...and "Did you try...?" My answers were always the same, "Tried that, did that, done that. Thank you."

I was very fortunate, I thought, to possess the sacred information that had been so secretly protected since my birth. Maybe it was a lesson that confirmed one could really obtain anything with genuine effort. It took all my will to eliminate the events of my journey from my thoughts while I waited on jewelry clients.

Later in the day I began to feel the same familiar hollowness in my soul. I wasn't satisfied with the court summary, and I still had the desperate need to see and know my birthmother. I became nauseated with the fear that this could really be the end of the saga. The last sentence echoed eerily in my mind --"It was felt that Mrs. Price was not telling the truth."

The phone rang. I answered.

"Hello, Mr. Watson?" said a middle-aged male voice.

"Yes."

"Mike, my name is Ernie Sullivan from the Noblesville Daily Topics newspaper. We were given a copy of a document that was pinned on the courthouse door." He spoke with a smile.

"Yes, sir, that was me."

"Mike, we were told by the ladies in the courthouse you were searching for your birthmother, whom you feel might have lived here in Noblesville. Actually, I believe you left a copy all over town, didn't you?" he chuckled.

"Yeah, I guess I did."

"We would like to do a story about your search, and maybe if there is anyone here who knows about your mother, they can contact you."

"That would be great!" My spirit awakened. I sensed someone was on my side.

I hung up the telephone with renewed aspiration. The missing piece of my identity would soon be inserted into the puzzle of the past. Someone would call from the coverage, I was sure. Maybe it would be my birthmother herself. The reporter said the article would appear in Wednesday's paper and that he would send me a copy.

No one called Wednesday. On Thursday I got a manila envelope from the Noblesville newspaper. I opened it quickly and the front page blazoned in bold typeface: *"Where Is Michael Watson's Family?"*

Everything was there, including the marriage, divorce, and other data from the court summary. Toward the bottom, it read, "In a telephone interview, Mike said he would like to hear from anyone who can provide information regarding his mother, father, half brother, or their families." It also gave my home address and the telephone number of the newspaper.

I waited patiently for the next week. I called my parents from work every day to ask them if I received any mail or if anybody called. The news was published again the following Wednesday, *"The Search Continues - No Success Yet."* The employees encouraged me by saying someone would contact me just from the publicity: *Somebody will know somebody who knows somebody.* Three weeks passed. Then four.

But nobody called.

Another month passed. The excitement of the preceding weeks had settled and life resumed its normal state at the Watson household. I knew that the words printed on the court summary were like tiny keys that could unlock the secrets of the past. That document remained in a dark and top secret file, hidden from anyone's eyes for a quarter of a century. I knew this had become a very personal journey. Everyone was entertained by my burden, but no one shared my obsession.

I browsed through my worn *ALMA* book. I imagined my birthmother being as close as a local telephone call. She had now metamorphosed into a real person. Before my last trip to Indianapolis she was a mythical being, having no shape or substance. Interestingly, as a child I could easily create a mental picture of the *boogieman.* It was a monster that dwelled in the closets of little children. It had black fur, fang-like teeth, and diagonal red slits for eyes that glowed in the dark. My birthmother, on the other hand, was forever an apparition in my dreams. From the court summary, Betty Price had finally taken on a physical form, "...a small woman, wore her hair in a pig-tail."

I went to the bathroom mirror and peered so close that the glass fogged from my breath. Touching my face, I envisioned my features softened, with a dark brown ponytail. My birthmother's eyes were very dark like mine, I imagined, but with the underlying expression of sorrow. I imagined her walking down the gusty streets of Indianapolis with her head down. As her hair trailed behind her, she wondered about the child she never saw: the Relinquished One who would now be another's Chosen One. She justified forsaking her son in the name of love. She had her words prepared if I ever knocked on her shabby door, "I wanted to keep you so much, my son, but because I didn't have enough money to support even myself, I had no choice but to give you away. Please don't hate me."

I removed my hands from my face and returned to the *ALMA* book. A paragraph mentioned how to obtain birth certificates and said that they include the *maiden* name of the mother. I figured I could obtain this if I pretended to be my half-brother. Then I would be able to find my grandparents, her closest relatives. I went to work on my old typewriter.

Indiana State Department of Health
Vital Records Division

Please send me a copy of my birth certificate.  Enclosed is a money order for $10.00.

Mother's name:  Betty Price
Father's name: Floyd Price
Born:  1953
Place: Marion County

Sincerely,
Michael David Price

I realized how ignorant I was as I typed, and thought I would be laughed at for omitting the month and day Michael David Price was born. The court summary said she was from Plymouth. Although that statement could have been false, I nevertheless increased my chances by typing variations of the letter, including Marshall and Hamilton counties.

I mailed them and waited. During the next few days I received reply letters that responded virtually the same: 'In order to obtain a birth certificate, it is necessary to include your mother's <u>maiden</u> name. We are returning your money order. Thank you.'

As I crumbled the last reply into the trash, I thought of life's contradictions, such as not being able to get a job without experience for that job, or not obtaining credit unless you already have credit, or *knowing your mother's maiden name* before you can *know your mother's maiden name!*

Several months later I repeated my request for a birth certificate using my own name and birth date. It was possible, I heard, that a negligent clerk could mistakenly pull the unamended copy and send it to me. I received my very official-looking amended birth certificate shortly thereafter from the Vital Records Division, pretending to convey that my biological parents were Martha and Stoy Watson.

Sometime later I wrote to the principal of Noblesville High School. I sent a copy of the court summary, saying I was hunting for my birthmother in his city. I politely asked him to scan the school's yearbooks and to see if there was a young girl named Betty that matched the description from the summary. I re-sent my letter a week later. I never did receive a reply, and figured they thought I was a lunatic.

Drearily, I ran out of clues. In 1984 I wrote the Marion County Department of Public Welfare.

ATTN: Child Welfare Division

Indianapolis, IN

I am an adoptee searching for my birthmother. Mrs. Mildred
Hardesty was the caseworker. This is my second request in asking
who has access to her records and whereabouts. I have a copy
of the original court summary. I must have additional information
in order to find her. Please respond.

And my answered letter:

Due to the gigantic storage problem of closed records, the older
ones have been destroyed. The information in our files regarding
the study our agency made for the Marion County Probate Court
is one of those expunged.

Your placement was a non-agency adoptive placement which
means that only one contact, the office interview, was had with
your biological mother. The totality of information, which our
caseworker obtained, would have been included in this report.

Mrs. Hardesty retired over sixteen years ago. If she produced
the same amount of studies as our present caseworkers, she
would have completed more than 200 per year. There is no way
that anything could be added to the data in the report she made
to the court on June 16, 1958.

Although someone once told me that there is a great joy
when a social worker places a child, I also wondered if they failed
to realize that adoptees eventually grow up and desire to know
something as primal as who gave birth to them.

I remembered how the Noblesville Daily Topics caused such a front-page commotion about my trip to their town. I then became amazed, thinking about being in the *Indianapolis Star.* Millions of people would read it, and it would be quite impossible to not find someone who knew about my beginnings. I dialed a reporter, trying to persuade her to write an article. She responded apologetically that adoptees looking for their birthparents are not really in the public's interest at the time, but for a small fee, I could place an ad in the classifieds. I stifled a laugh before hanging up, imagining the headline, "Boy Looking For Mother. If you gave birth to me, please call."

*"Whenever I touch a flower, I touch the sun yet I do not get burned. When I touch the flower, I touch a cloud without flying to the sky....If you really touch one flower deeply, you touch the whole cosmos."*

**Cultivating the Mind of Love. Thich Nhat Hahn. Permission of Parallax Press, Berkeley, California.**

## 12. In Search of California

In 1985 I married a young girl named Ellen. We had been dating for the previous eight months. Coincidentally, two weeks later I was asked to manage one of Shalaar's divisions in Overland Park, Kansas. Ellen and I would fly there shortly afterwards for an orientation of the new position.

Overland Park was over five hundred miles from New Albany. Until then, I had never ventured very far from home. I realized that any ensuing attempts in my search would be stifled from the further distance. I would be pushed farther from my bloodroots. Nevertheless, it was time to become completely self-sufficient, for I had just recently been weaned from the nourishment of my parents' refrigerator. I now had a companion to begin a new life in a new world.

My supervisor-to-be and his wife met us at the Country Club Plaza in Kansas City. His name was Hank Scarly, a short, fast talker who avoided direct eye contact. Scarly flagged down one of the black horse and buggies that rode tourists through the plaza. Scarly and his wife enjoyed the view from the front seat. Ellen and I crouched uncomfortably in the back. As Scarly mumbled passing points of interest, my new bride and I were content with just absorbing the almost magical surroundings. We went to a restaurant afterwards.

"So, what... do you think about Kansas, Michael?" the supervisor garbled just before swallowing a bite of filet mignon.

"I love it." I exclaimed.

"Would you and your wife enjoy working here?"

"Oh, yeah. It would be really great, " I said.

"What do you say about starting next week?"

There it was. The infamous sales close. Spoken at that strategic moment after I shoveled a large spoonful of mint ice cream into my mouth. The initial salary was lower than I expected. The pressure was on. I gulped hard. "I'm very sorry, Mr. Scarly." The coldness froze my brain. "I don't think I will be able to come out here and work for so little money."

Scarly's eyes became unexpectedly wide from surprise. He fumbled with his spoon and asked worriedly, "Michael, what do you mean? We are offering you much more than you're making in Louisville? Think about the bonuses you'll make as a manager."

"That's true, but I've studied the cost of living here." I spoke confidently, even though I had conducted no such research. "Expenses are higher here than in Kentucky and Indiana. Utilities are higher because of severe winters and hot summers. Plus Kansas has higher taxes on income and automobiles. I would have to receive a higher salary before I could consider your offer."

The supervisor remained silent. I continued stuffing myself with ice cream. His thoughts were cellophane. Here he was, handing his credit card to the waiter for an astronomical amount. He would also have to pay our night at the hotel. And lastly, the expense of air travel would be in vain.

"Let's go into the corridor and talk, Michael," he said with a grinch-like smile.

Though I hadn't finished my dessert, I followed him where we could talk in private. From a distance, observers noticed our animated arm and hand gestures, signifying an unsuccessful conference.

Ellen and I returned to Indiana, and received a phone call from the vice president two days later, compromising the beginning wages. We agreed to the higher earnings and flew back to Overland Park.

I had long accepted the uniqueness of being adopted and the intermittent curiosity of my roots had become a way of life. Sometimes I expressed feelings of void to my wife and the new employees. I wondered if my biological parents were in the jewelry business or were musically inclined. I wished I could thank them for the talents that they genetically bestowed to me. My eternal quest slowly disappeared, however, after I assumed the two simultaneous titles of husband and jewelry store manager.

Less than a year later, Ellen called late at night to say she wasn't coming home. I sleepily rose from my pillow and asked if she still loved me. She said she didn't know. I asked if she still wanted to be married. She replied the same, and said she would come the next day to get her things while I was at work.

There was no familiar sound of television commercials as I entered the apartment the following evening, and the rooms had doubled in size from the removed furnishings. She had not even left a telephone number, and I never heard from her again.

I prayed selfishly for an answer. My ignorance of not knowing my destiny was more agonizing than being prepared for a life of loneliness in a city that was light years from the place in which I was raised and had declared as *home*.

I wept. From out of nowhere, I felt a serenity that penetrated my being. Although there was no actual voice or touch on my shoulder, a real presence swept a gentle wave of peace through me. My anguish miraculously disintegrated, and I was assured that there was nothing *ever* to be worried about. My faith eventually became unshaken that a higher purpose was planned for both of us.

We divorced a few months later. I attended a support group for those who had similar fates. It was an assembly of about twenty people, mostly women, who came to re-establish meaning in their lives. Some were victims of abuse or were emotionally wounded from infidelity, and one woman had been married for over twenty years. My preconceptions of eternal marital bliss became jangled and, *for better or worse*, it was difficult to erase the memories of my short-termed marriage. Maybe I directed feelings of confusion and tyranny toward my own staff. Maybe that was good, for the store surpassed its sales projections for ten months straight. My income soared, and the plump commissions endowed me with a house complete with mature trees. Shortly afterwards, as a final touch to the decoration of the driveway, I acquired a beautiful red sports car.

The next thing I remember is Hank Scarly escorting me outside the store. He admitted that although the store's performance never faltered, my divorce seemed to estrange me from the rest of the employees. He said many complained that I refused to pay attention to them when they spoke to me. The store's morale did seem to sink, but I never once thought I was a direct cause of a lack of team spirit.

Induced by Scarly to take a hefty pay cut, I transferred to an undesirable Shalaars across the state border in Missouri. It was in Krison's Square, a dilapidated shopping mall many miles from my new home. My manager title was stripped away.

Living in another land, I couldn't go crying back to Mom. The enigma was even more devastating than the divorce from Ellen, for I had been *married* to Shalaars for almost ten years. I was just starting to get over the tragedy of my short-lived marriage with the help of my friends at the support group, and now I was faced with another dilemma that would recreate a second divorce.

Multiple misfortunes seemed to pour from an unseen flask. Kansas dust and pollen tormented me, and I developed a horrible cough that seemed to linger forever. While completing the lengthy forms in the doctor's office, I remembered my previous visits for the removal of wisdom teeth and stitching my split chin from a poolside injury. The blanks would always ask the same questions, like "What is your race?" or, "Important- In your family, are there any cases of heart disease, epilepsy, diabetes, or high blood pressure?" I could never truthfully answer a single question. Instead, I would write "adopted" and ditto marks to the end of the form.

The following months I tried to ascertain my exact Earth-Time position and reviewed my talents. I had no wife, no children, and no work place that I felt part of. I was relatively free from obligations and could go anywhere I chose. On the other hand, I *did* have a mortgage, and monthly bills from utility companies, insurance collectors, and from the bank for the little red car. My debts soon outgrew my reduced salary.

My passion was the diamond business. I felt worthy when helping a couple select a diamond ring that would symbolize their commitment to each other, a union which I privately hoped would last a long time.

One evening I unfolded a map of the United States. I could go anywhere, I reasoned. I never liked remote areas, like the small farm in Indiana, and I always despised scraping ice from windshields and shoveling snow. I placed my fingers near Southern California. Although I had never been there, I imagined the palm trees and warm climate. I caught myself smiling, and mentally created my destiny for the next world. *Believe in yourself and all things are possible.* I remembered Mom's words.

Krison's Square drew patrons who would rather steal jewelry than buy it, and the security personnel would always be toting those caught in the act with handcuffs down the walkway. The days went by slowly, and I tried to awaken myself whenever the new manager passed. Any asking price beyond one hundred dollars made customers think twice. During breaks I scanned the job classifieds.

I mailed several resumes to the Golden State. The few prospective employers who replied said that there was no consideration for employment unless they first met the applicant. The jewelry business was based on trust, they explained, and it would be impossible to hire anyone from a mere written description or telephone conversation.

My funds continued to shrink and I relinquished many personal belongings. After much grief, I put my house and car up for sale. I told Scarly that I was going to get a less expensive auto and rent an apartment. I was not lying, but I failed to tell him I was planning on moving to the west coast.

During lunch I would sneak to the public phone booth and retrieve a list of California jewelry companies that I had stashed in my pocket. They all responded the same, and I finally realized the necessity of applying in person. I purchased a dirty, brown-colored Mustang that had twice the mileage of my red car and accepted the first offer on my house.

Although Mom and Dad didn't agree with everything I did, they were the people I loved the most. Whether they approved or not, I always shared my dreams with them. I had learned to despise rotary telephones, and it felt nice to dial my familiar home number from the push buttons.

"Mom," I began, I'm moving to California. Don't worry about me."

"California? My Lord, Michael! Why are you going to California?" Mom was always the one who answered the phone even though Dad would probably be sitting right next to it. "Answer the phone, Veeler!" I imagined him saying before Mom picked up.

"There's nothing left for me out here, Mom. I've given this much thought. I'll get a job there. I'll be fine."

"Michael...me and your daddy would *never* get a chance to see you anymore! California? Who do you know in California?"

"Nobody," I admitted.

"Michael, I know you don't like being told what to do. Lord knows you never want to listen to your mom. But..." I listened patiently for what I knew was coming next. "Have you thought about who in the world will help you move all your furniture? What are you going to do when you get out there? My word, Michael, work is hard to find. What if you can't get a job? Then what are you going to do?"

"Mom. I love you. You'll never have to worry about me. Remember how you taught me *all things are possible?*" Then I remembered it was actually Mom who indirectly encouraged me to obtain the impossible: the adoption court summary.

"Michael, please give this some more thought, honey," she implored, ignoring my question. "I know you are smart, but that doesn't mean that there are any jobs in California to be had. Oh, boy. Wait till your Dad hears about this. We'll worry to death about you."

After a few minutes we hung up.

I had accumulated a four-week vacation and without wasting time, I set up several employment interviews. On the first day of my vacation, unbeknownst to Scarly or anyone at Shalaars, I flew to Los Angeles.

I sat alone on the plane, mostly just staring out the window. I suppose my actions were quite preposterous, for I really did not know a single person in the state of California. Just as ridiculously, I possessed a confidence that had surfaced from somewhere in my past. As I dreamily gazed into the clouds, my mind wandered back in time. Although Mom taught me to believe in myself, I never really knew my potential. In the ninth grade, the school sponsored a spelling contest for the whole student body. Since I had a knack for English, I channeled all of my energy into becoming a champion. My birthparents could have been geniuses, I always thought, and maybe, somewhere down deep, they could have bestowed that genius in me.

Mom drilled me until I memorized every word. I don't remember being nervous in front of one thousand eyes, or beside contest rivals. I had no fear of erring because I lived every word, and even though I didn't have a clue of their definitions, I could clearly visualize the correctly spelled letters in my brain.

I came in first place, gave a quick bow to the audience and was awarded a pin-on medal with a dingy yellow finish. Whether it was inborn genius or faith, Mom's theory was proven right, and my newfound self-esteem hoisted me onto the road in which the sign read:

I am adopted. I am important.

I am the *Chosen One.*

"The captain has asked that all passengers remain in their seats until we land." The blaring announcement jolted my trance. My life was unfolding on this very day, I had convinced myself. I dreamed about a tropical climate, new friends, and the challenge of braving a new world.

A nervous throb emerged in my throat as the wheels bumped the ground. At the baggage claim, I had never before seen such a mixture of nationalities. Hundreds of passengers, none of whom even remotely resembled me, were gathered around the luggage tram waiting for the split second to snatch the handles of their belongings that zipped in front of them.

After a few interviews, it was clear that I would have to list a reference. I called the manager at Krison's Square from a clamorous phone booth:

"Jason, this is Michael," I said loudly.

"Hello, Michael!" I always liked Jason Crandall. "Enjoying your vacation?"

"Jason, I need a reference," I said louder, plugging one ear tightly."

"I figured this would happen sooner or later, Michael. You know I can only say great things about you. Why is it so noisy?"

"I'm in downtown L.A."

"L.A.! And we thought you were looking for an apartment over here." And after a brief interchange, Jason said, "Michael, you have my warmest blessings, and I wish you the best of luck. Feel free to use my name anytime you wish."

"Thanks, Jason," I said. "You're great. Goodbye."

On the third appointment the interviewer said Halbert's Jewelers needed a salesperson at one of their locations fifty miles south of Los Angeles. I drove with a map I discovered in the back seat of the rental and braved the freeway swollen with thousands of cars. I exited onto a much more peaceful street, then found my destination at a jewelry store in an elegant mall in Costa Mesa. The opening dialogue was dry, but after the supervisor discovered I was a gemologist, he asked me to start in a week.

I certainly could not survive the high rent district of Costa Mesa, and noticed the rates seemed to decrease the farther north I drove. I finally put a deposit on a budget apartment in a Hispanic community of Santa Ana, and flew back to Kansas to pack my meager possessions. I rented a huge bright yellow Ryder truck, christened her *Jasmine*, and connected the heavily-dented Mustang to the rear. Bidding farewell to friends and neighbors, I began a three-day journey into an unknown galaxy.

America was so lonely. My radio did not work. My mind wandered infinitely. I thought about every event from my childhood until the present. I remembered Veronica Walsh, an employee I had hired in Overland Park. I always told Veronica that life was like a triangle, in which humans are always striving to reach a higher level. Her side was that life was like a circle, where we all eventually come to the same point from which we originated. Neither one of us could convincingly argue our viewpoints, but we always respected each other's opinions.

The mountains of Colorado dimly came into focus. As *Jasmine* sped nearer, the evening grew dark, and the mountains eventually disappeared into the blackness. It wasn't until morning, while surrounded by gigantic red rocks in Utah, that I awakened from my weeklong stupor. The thought of the painful separation from Ellen writhed into my mind. I thundered affirmations over *Jasmine's* raucous grunting that my marriage did not fail, but was indeed a success for the short term it lasted. I remembered when I prayed for an answer, and I remembered the *Understanding* I received as a divine reply.

It seemed that the largest portion of my life had always been such a solitary quest, and I suddenly realized my aloneness. If Veronica Walsh's life-circle theory was correct, I would never be able to completely fulfill my life, for how could I return to the same point that I started if I never had an origin? As the thought of my birthmother crept into my mind, I again realized that I was denied a place on the X and Y axis of my human creation.

The compelling lure of the Pacific eventually aroused my senses again. I realized that I had nowhere in life to go but upward. I had no past, but I had the will to create my destiny. The large wheel in my grip transformed into the helm of my future. I could steer it left or steer it right. But for now, I continued to travel linearly in the snorting yellow time machine, with the sun at my back in the morning and blaring in my face in the evening. New Albany is where I was raised, I thought, but California would be my home.

On the third day I arrived in Santa Ana and plowed into the entrance of my new apartment complex with the old Mustang trailing behind the truck. Jumping to the ground, I gave my legs a good stretch and ambled to the management office for the key to my second-story room. The key said 902, but I knocked on door 903.

"Hi," I began, My name is Michael." A handsome, dark-skinned young man answered. "I'm going to be your new neighbor. If there's anything I can do for you, just let me know."

"Cómo?" was the reply. Unfortunately, my foreign language classes never included Spanish. Then four other young men appeared at the entrance. One who could speak better English than the others emerged in front.

"Hi. How are you?" he said.

"Great. Thank you. I was just telling your friend that I will be your new neighbor. If there is anything I can do for you or your friends, just let me know." I repeated my sales close word for word.

"Nice to meet you." Miguel welcomed a friendly hand. "If we do something for you, let us know too."

"Thank you. Do you and your friends like pizza?" I spoke slowly, with plenty of pauses, while waving exaggerated gestures.

I was renowned for that anyway, and Dad said if I were born without arms I wouldn't be able to talk.

"Sí . Yes," Miguel and two others nodded.

"If you can help me move a few of my things into my apartment, I will buy two large pizzas for all of us." I motioned again, maintaining a brisk smile although weary from the trip.

"Sure." Miguel looked toward the others for mutual consent. "We help you."

"Great. Let's go!" My sales wrap up.

As the boys scurried around the corner, they seemed less enthusiastic when they saw *Jasmine* taking up most of the parking lot. Nevertheless, Miguel clapped his hands as one does at the beginning of a laborious but necessary job, like mowing the lawn. One by one, each boy grabbed a furniture leg and hauled it into apartment 902. They never once faltered in their pace. I worked equally hard.

Returning for the fifth armload I noticed an attractive, golden-skinned girl with long, almost onyx black hair, walking hurriedly in the same direction I was. Thinking I might not ever get another chance to talk to her I seized her attention.

"Hi, my name is Michael. I'm your new neighbor. If there's any..."

"Yeah. Okay. Thank you." She smiled pleasantly without listening. "I have to go. Bye." Then she left.

Her abruptness startled me, and her response was that of one who tries to get rid of a pesky salesperson. I realized my greetings were becoming stale. I shrugged and continued toward the truck.

An hour later the Latino gentlemen and I all sat down to the now reassembled massive oak dining room table. I was hungry, but too fatigued to eat. The young boys looked physically fit and unaffected from making so many trips up and down the steps. I felt like a sweat-soaked sponge. Fulfilling my promise, we consumed both pizzas and several beers.

My timing was right on schedule, and I went to work the next day. I awoke early to the California sun that brightened the walls of my new bedroom. My bones ached. I dressed in a fresh suit for the first time in a week and left for Halbert's Jewelers.

As I returned to the apartment in the evening, I noticed the pretty girl from the day before. She was peeking out from the door below mine. Another woman's face appeared in the opening, motioning for me to come. The woman introduced the mystery Guatemalan girl.

Her name was Maria del Carmen. This time she looked into my eyes. When she spoke, she delighted all of my senses. She was wondrously the first girl in California who interested me.

Other than a cardboard slice of pepperoni and cheese, there was no food. I invited Carmen to the grocery store--our first date. Excited as unattended children in a toy store, we filled the grocery cart past its rim without once looking at the individual prices. We talked so incessantly while driving back that we failed to see that the stoplights had changed to green. On three occasions the cars behind us beeped impatiently. Returning to the apartment, after helping me nail the final painting on the wall, Carmen introduced me to the delectable dining pleasure of fried banana, black beans, and corn tortillas.

I soon adapted to my new lifestyle, and I just as quickly began a love affair with the coastal breeze and mountains that I summoned from my apartment window. I lived every moment with the immense appreciation of being alive. Even though I cherished each day like a long-awaited vacation, I squeezed every ounce of pleasure from free time by escaping to the beach. There the warm sand massaged my back and waves climbed just inches below my feet. The gentle roar of the ocean would perform stereophonically while the Pacific sun caressed my face and body.

With my new girlfriend and employer, the quest for my roots dissolved. I enjoyed the fast pace of Southern California. When highways were not jammed, automobiles seemed to travel at an average speed of twenty miles per hour over the posted limits. I would help jewelry customers by day, then walk on the beach with Carmen in the evening, using a blanket to shield ourselves from the cool ocean wind.

Carmen made me feel young and alive. English soon replaced her native Spanish dialect, and she became prolific in this second language much faster than I did hers. I remember the excitement of learning new words as we slowly mouthed the syllables. My goal of rehumanizing myself in a new world was being fulfilled, and the joy of being with Carmen healed every wound I suffered from the past.

## 13. The Legend of Gallery of Diamonds

It was 1991. Two years had passed. I had always dreamed of opening a diamond jewelry store, and squirreled away a portion of my paychecks in case opportunity knocked. I read business books while basking on the beach, returning them to the library bearing pages smudged from suntan oil. Unfortunately, the economy had become sluggish and jewelry sales had dwindled mercilessly. Halbert's Jewelers implied rumors of a company takeover and, just before their doors closed forever, I escaped to a rival across the mall. Then *that* store filed Chapter Eleven: then Thirteen. The lighted marquis of the entrance quickly changed names, and I found myself working for a third employer. There was nothing that could shock me about the accelerated transformations of my California world.

For sure, the jewelry market had hit bottom. It couldn't get worse. There was nowhere to go but up.

Now was the time to open a new business!

I sold personal belongings to raise capital and was convinced it was passion, blended with honesty, that was the secret to success. Venture capitalists ignored the small dreams of a single jewelry outlet. Banks considered a loan if one were *already* in business for at least two years. Nevertheless, with meager funds,

*Gallery of Diamonds* was born in Costa Mesa with a metal safe and security alarm system, and a humble inventory of about twenty rings and chains. There was certainly no fury of holiday shoppers during that founding year, and the fledgling firm produced only moderate sales. Carmen and I tossed flyers even in drizzling rain, and advertised till the checking account dipped below one hundred dollars. We had to do something different-- something no one thought of before, something that would bring more customers. Then the idea struck. I would give a diamond to a student who would write the most heartfelt essay about his or her mom. Although there was little room left for wondering about my biological beginnings, the contest would give kids a chance to express their love and appreciation for their own moms. I called a few schools and invited kids to write about *Why Mom Deserves a Diamond*. The winner would receive a quarter-carat diamond to give to mom on Mother's Day. No one knew it at the time, as Margaret Ketchersid presented the winning diamond to her mother on *Diamond Day*, but the course of history would forever be changed in the way thousands of kids could honor their moms.

## 14. Lady by the Lake

The following July I married Carmen. We had a small ceremony on the beach, where majestic crags protrude from the crashing waves. It was a fitting place, for we had spent so much precious time there holding hands on the wet sand. Her dress gleamed bright in the sun.

Of course, marriage would eventually mean children. What would I tell them? Wouldn't I have an obligation to disclose their origination? And how could I do that if *I* didn't know? During a quiet moment at the jewelry store, I referred back to the original court summary and read it again. My memories rewound a decade, when I had shared the summary with Mom and Dad. Noblesville had always been a physical place on the map. Plymouth, however, was always mysterious to me, quite possibly contrived as the city my birthmother was from, and it was even more obscure now that I lived nearly two thousand miles away from it. Then again, I was disappointed in myself for not attempting to explore this area earlier in my life.

I spoke to a newspaper editor from Plymouth. A week later the newspaper displayed on its first page, *"Watson Searches for Mother."* There was a photo of me that I had sent along with a few hand-written paragraphs and concluded with my work telephone number.

This time somebody called.

"Is this Michael Watson?" an elderly and faraway voice asked.

"Yes, that's me."

"My name is Margy Flora and I read the article in this morning's paper, and I just wanted to say that I knew your birthmother."

My heart jumped. "Y...you did?"

"She's not living anymore, I'm sorry to say, but I just want you to know that Betty Price was a very fine lady. We went to school together many years ago. At our last class reunion, she was listed as deceased, but I wanted to send you a photo of her taken by the lake. I will send it to you so you will know what she looked like."

"You really knew her?"

"Oh, yes, dear. I'm going to send you this picture so you will always remember your birthmother as the beautiful lady by the lake."

"How old is she, I mean, was she?"

"I don't know when she passed away. She was a year younger than me. So she would have been seventy-three years old now."

I raised an eyebrow and twisted my mouth towards the side of my face. I knew this warmhearted lady was getting ready to send a photo of another Betty Price, for if she would have been seventy-three than I would have miraculously aged sixteen years. Nevertheless, I gave her my address and two days later I received a black and white photo of an attractive lady posing in front of what seemed more like a duck pond. It wasn't my mother. That's the last I heard from anyone in Plymouth.

Southern California had been deluged with every catastrophe known, including earthquakes, fires, floods, and riots. Although I had personally escaped each danger, I could not escape the peril of my own biological ignorance. I realized I had made an isolated journey to the point of no return. The desire to know my bloodroots was far beyond a curiosity. It now consumed me.

I heard of a service that, for a small fee, would generate a computer listing of any name in the United States. I sent my check and three days later I received a report of over three hundred and fifty Michael Prices in the country. One of those Michaels, I had hoped, would be my half-brother. Finding him would not only be an easier task, but it would also be the key to finding my birthmother. I made a few hundred copies of the court summary I had guarded like a precious diamond and included this form letter in my mass mailing:

October 30, 1993

Dear Mr. Price,

Please look over this court summary. There is a possibility that you could be related to me. Read the section that says "Mother of Child." If your mother's name was Betty Price or if there are any names, dates, or places that are familiar, call me collect.

I was adopted in 1958. I have been searching for my natural family my entire life. If nothing sounds familiar, please pass this on to someone else in your family.

I neatly folded the letters and inserted them into about two hundred envelopes. When the mail carrier noticed that all were addressed to Mr. Michael Price, he shrugged his shoulders, shook his head, and stashed them under his arm as he left in a bewildered state.

I waited patiently for return mail or telephone calls. Maybe my half-brother received the letter but thought the whole thing was a prank, or perhaps didn't want to reveal himself.

A Michael Price with a pronounced southern drawl called on the third day. Because the jewelry store was busy I put him on hold and promised to return right away. After several minutes, I returned and thanked him for hanging on. He confirmed receiving my letter, but apologized that he was not related to me. Not only was that the wrong answer, I was also aggravated because he took my advice and called collect. I thanked him and replaced the receiver with a harder than average force.

## 15. The Mystery Clue

A recent amendment in Indiana allowed adoptees and birthparents to complete a form from the State Department of Health, the *Indiana Adoption History Registration*, which would give consent for the searching parties to exchange identifying or non-identifying information. I remembered that I had sent that form one year ago and also that I had not received a reply. Either my birthmother did not want to find me, she was dead, or she wasn't familiar with such a service. I hoped for the latter.

At home I fetched a folder that was always kept in a locked file and burrowed through the myriad of papers that I had toted across the country. Inside lay the barely legible notes from the calls I had made at the elderly couple's house on North Delaware Street. There were also the phone numbers of three erroneous Michael Prices I resisted throwing away. There was one Michael Price that I must have bothered at least three times. The last time I called he said, 'Look, pal, I'm not your brother, okay?'

I clutched the two postcards of Community Hospital, each being twenty years apart, and also the three, wrinkled blue folders Mom had given me as a child. I cautiously read every word of the court summary. Carmen fell asleep beside me as I memorized every word.

The next morning I called the county building in Indianapolis. I begged the clerk to see if they had any information besides the original court summary.

"What form are you referring to?" the lady who answered asked.

"It says case number E38-02892,'" I answered, reading the top of the document.

"How did you get that form?" the lady demanded.

"Judge Jameson gave it to me many years ago."

"You're not supposed to have that form," she said sternly, and then I wondered if she expected me to mail it back. She continued to say that another judge had taken Judge Jameson's place and that they were very strict about releasing information.

I hung up. Although I had been dawdling at a dead end for nearly two decades, I felt blessed to own a trace of genealogical evidence that many adoptees are refused.

Over the past weeks, an anonymous lady had been sending me letters of advice. I largely ignored the mystery woman, but I followed one of her clues: *Get a copy of your birthmother's wedding license application.* Although I had previously failed at that endeavor, I had never queried other than Marion or Hamilton counties. That evening I questioned if Noblesville was a place my birthmother only pretended to be from to ensure I would never find her.

I commenced a new expedition. There were nearly one hundred counties in Indiana. I retrieved the address of every courthouse, and the following morning I typed a short request:

Please search and send a copy of the marriage license application for:

Floyd Price and Betty _____ (maiden name unknown)

DATE: Approximately December 29, 1951.

If cannot find, please check between years of 1951-1956. If there is a charge for this service, please let me know.

Crisp pages spewed from the printer. I spent most of the morning stuffing, stamping, and rubber-banding the letters into a pile before the mail carrier arrived.

My request was identical to that which I had made many years ago except that I expanded the market one-hundred-fold to the entire state of Indiana. My scheme was that if I failed in my home state, I would continue mass marketing letters to every single courthouse in the United States if necessary.

From the increasing growth of the *Why Mom Deserves a Diamond* contest, receiving huge quantities of mail had become routine. As I sorted letters into separate stacks of Mother's Day essays, bills, and junk mail, I found three letters from Indiana courthouses. Using my right thumb as a letter opener, I yanked out the contents of each envelope.

During the previous weeks I had been sent copies of many wedding license applications from different counties, none of which seemed to have any significance with my genesis. But the third envelope with a return address of Putnam County stirred my attention, for the headline read, "Application is hereby made for a License for the Marriage of: Floyd Price to Betty Stewart." As I veered downwards, the issue date was December 29, 1951--the precise wedding date mentioned in the court summary.

The shock of seeing a statistical match made me feel weak. It would be much easier to regard the incident as a hoax, I thought, but the coincidence was too obvious. Along with the lifelong habit of searching, I had become comfortable in gathering erroneous information. It was uncomfortable, however, to once again hold a document that was somehow associated with my introduction to this world.

I held the record open at arms length and viewed it like a student of abstract art. The blanks were filled with exaggerated spirals and words were slanted to the right. Because of my left-handedness, I always slanted the opposite direction. The first letter of each word was strongly accented followed by much smaller lowercase letters. Small p's, g's, and y's sometimes looped down three or four lines. I deducted that it was a young female that filled out the entire parchment, and I was overwhelmed by the certainty of seeing my birthmother's penmanship for the first time. The style of the handwriting was my first glimpse into her creative past. If my search had truly come to an end, I tried to convince myself to feel fortunate in possessing another artifact that so many adoptees are denied, like the handwriting swirls of one's birthmother that float on a piece of paper.

I looked again at the name of the future bride on the right corner. Her maiden name was Stewart. The application was divided into two columns for each applicant: left for the male, right for the female. I peered down the right column and continued reading. In the blank asking the full Christian and surname of father was written Otis Stewart. His occupation said state highway employee--my Grandfather! Until that moment I had never conceptualized another grandpa, like Mom's dad, who died when I was a teenager. Grandma died when I was a child. The only thing I remembered is her instructing me how to put on my undershirt, asserting that the tag must go in the back.

Further down, the full Christian and maiden name of mother specified Hattie Murphy, my Grandmother! My personal revelation intensified as I uncovered the identities of three relatives.

I scanned unsuccessfully for the word Noblesville. But filled in the blank, *where born*, was the name of another town with the same suffix--Coatesville. So that's where she was from! I involuntarily made a quick turn as if to tell somebody the news until I realized I was alone. Then I became aware of standing in the mortal silence. The whir of computer hard drives, fax machines, and the rumble of the jewelry polisher had not yet commenced. Hurling toward the desk drawer, I fetched a pocket-sized map of the United States, dotted with only the major cities.

I called my next door friend, Daniel. Daniel was a genius in world geography and was a forerunner to Internet access. I told him about my discovery and asked him to find Coatesville on the web. After pressing a few keys he said it was a very small town thirty miles west of Indianapolis with a population of three hundred and fifty.

I thanked him, hung up, and fiddled with the application for several minutes. I called Carmen, stuttered my excitement into the tiny holes of the mouthpiece and hung up without saying goodbye.

Then I called Mom. Other than the physical act of giving birth to me, she had not only been my mother in every sense of the word, but also my friend. As her telephone rang I hoped that the combined words intermingled in my mouth and brain would be delivered coherently. For a brief second I realized the ridiculousness of saying, 'Hi, mother, I found my mother.'

She picked up on the third ring. "Mom, I found my birthmother!" I blurted triumphantly.

"What do you mean, you *found* her?" She spoke firmly, but dazed.

"Her name was Betty Stewart. That was her maiden name." Then I realized that it would be impossible for her to share my excitement, at least at the same intensity as myself. As I waited for her response, I also realized that this victorious day for me might have also been the day she had dreaded since I was born. I proceeded to tell her about the morning's mail.

"Stoy, honey, Michael found his birthmother," she spoke with a monotone toward Dad's chair. Dad's muffled voice echoed from the background. "What are you going to do now, I mean, just be careful, Michael, whatever you do."

"I'll let you know as soon as I find out more," I answered. "After all, this information is forty-three years old. I might not find anyone. I love you."

"I love you, too. Just be careful. Goodbye."

I could not concentrate on the jewelry business the entire day. I was certain this form would unlock the vaulted door to the past. I felt driven to journey to Coatesville by plane or by foot, but gradually composed myself and tried to allow logic to take the place of emotion. I had waited far too long, I thought, to allow all my years of genealogical exploration to become vain.

I had heard of a Master Death file, a retrieval system in which one can verify if an individual has died. I never made use of such a service before, realizing that my birthmother's last name would have surely changed. Or maybe it was because I was afraid that she very well *was* dead. I made a quick pencil calculation and ascertained that she would presently be fifty-nine.

I called a researcher that had access to death records in Indiana and gave the information she requested: which were the names, Otis and Hattie Stewart; the town, Coatesville; and a parameter of possible dates of death. The rapid pecking of the researcher's fingers on her computer keypad sounded like Morse Code at hyper speed.

"No one listed as Hattie Stewart, sir," she responded. My heart drummed when I realized that my grandmother must still be alive. "Let me try Otis Stewart." The pecking continued. "I have three listings for O. Stewart," the researcher said. "And, yes, ...*tapk tapk*...here we are,...*tapk*, Stewart, Otis died in Coatesville,

Indiana in May, 1987." She spoke without emotion or remorse. Of course, it was not her job to console mourners. To her I was just an everyday caller, pursuing the archives of the past. She had no idea that the persons I was searching for were the biological grandparents I had never met and that I never knew existed before I opened this morning's mail.

I felt ill. I had already begun to visualize my grandfather as a hardworking citizen who was likable to all who met him, and now he was dead. As far as I was concerned, he had died right there as I held the telephone receiver against my ear.

"The charge is ten dollars," she said, interrupting my train of thought. "Please mail me a check, and I will send you a full report."

I obeyed by involuntarily reaching for my checkbook after I replaced the receiver. My grandfather had died six years ago, and I had never even met him.

At closing, I went home and carefully handed Carmen the document as if it were one of the Dead Sea Scrolls. I reread the notes in my personal files to confirm I had really found my blood family. Everything matched except the name of the town. It now seemed certain that my birthmother intended to camouflage her trail, for Coatesville was located many miles on an opposite side of Indianapolis. I had been searching in the wrong place for the past twenty years.

Carmen and I reviewed the application from the sofa. The phone rang.

"Michael, did you find out anything else?" Mom said.

"No, Mom. Except that my grandfather is dead," I answered.

"What do you mean, your grandfather's dead?" she asked, confused. I proceeded to explain.

"Honey, me and your daddy have been looking on the map, and we can't find Coatesville." At my current age of thirty-six, I still had parents that considered themselves my mommy and daddy. "There is one place that looks like...C.T.S.V." I could tell she was straining her eyes as she pronounced each letter "...but I don't see no Coatesville."

"That's it, Mom. It's a very small town, smaller than its own name."

"You're not going there...to Coatesville...are you?" Like all moms, I suppose mine knew me better than anyone else on earth, and she also knew that no city would obstruct my endless quest.

"No, Mom. Don't worry. How do we even know anyone's still living there?" I heard her sigh with relief, and we bade each other goodnight. Then I realized what I had just said. I wondered if anyone genetically related to me actually did still live in a town which had a population less than half the number of apartments in my California complex. Although I never considered myself nomadic, I had already lived in three states and several cities. It was more likely, I imagined, that my biological family had probably already drifted to the ends of the earth.

## 16. Journey to the Black Hole

Waking early, I went to the store before dawn. It was a dangerous move. For security reasons, it is vital that more than one person opens or closes a jewelry store. Nevertheless, I double-bolted the door and notified the alarm company of my early arrival. I poured dark, Guatemalan beans into the Mr. Coffee and carried the marriage license copy to my chair.

I had never taken anyone's advice on hiring a private investigator, and now I was masquerading as one. Betty Price had finally been identified as the former Betty Stewart. If I had known her maiden name twenty years ago, I would have surely called every Stewart in the phone books of my past. I realized how fruitless it was to mangle my fingers from the old rotary phone from the elderly couple's home on North Delaware Street.

The first gulp of the aromatic brew offered a brilliant idea. Since I knew the date of my grandfather's death, all I had to do was find the obituary in the local newspaper. It would most likely list the survivors, including my birthmother, and also the state where they were currently living. I pushed a couple of numbers on my calculator and found that Betty would have been fifty-one years old. If I could read an obituary column, it would reveal her current married name. The most recent data I had ever uncovered about her, according to my worn court summary, was 'on September 15, 1955, she divorced Mr. Price.' Surely she would have remarried during the succeeding four decades, and quite possibly more than once.

My mind scrambled to devise a way to get a copy of a Coatesville community newspaper. I knew the month and year Otis passed away, but the researcher had no record of the exact day. Maybe their local paper was released weekly. But what if there were no copies? Surely the old publications would not be computerized. Coatesville was not like New York, for heaven's sake. Although the data I was seeking was only six years old, a town that minuscule might not religiously preserve the written records of its past. My mind rambled as I noticed myself creating my own obstacle course. The notion of speaking to the editor of the Coatesville newspaper was too obvious, and like the hopeless odds of winning the lottery, I never remembered obtaining anything of value from a simple phone call.

A scrolled piece of paper lay on the floor. It was a fax from Daniel who must have sent it during the night. Uncurling it, I read the headline: 'Coatesville Community Development Association. Welcome To Our Community.' Daniel had apparently conducted further research on the small town.

> The town of Coatesville originated sometime during the early 1850's. It was incorporated in 1909 and two years later the town built a school house.
>
> Coatesville was originally a village called West Milton. However, an early settler by the name of Henry Coates gave some land for the town site and because of his liberal offering the town was given the name Coatesville.
>
> When the Pennsylvania Railroad was completed, the town soon became a thriving community with a number of businesses ... There was a flour mill where the Elevator now stands, there was a tin and a plumbing shop, four doctor's

offices, two saloons, a picture show and numerous smaller businesses.

Coatesville has a very deep Christian heritage. In the early days, there was Methodist, Christian, Baptist, Primitive Baptist, and Quaker churches. All still remain except the Quaker Church.

The town of Coatesville was struck by a tornado on Good Friday, 1948. This was a massive storm that touched down just southwest of Fillmore and lifted off the ground at the west edge of Danville. The business district was devastated. Three of the four churches were destroyed completely.

From the destruction, a new town emerged with merchants and townsfolk of one mind to rebuild...

I fantasized about living in that village. If it were not for my adoption, I very well might still be there. At least I would have escaped that horrible calamity on Good Friday, which occurred ten years before I was born. I might have been a farmer producing grain or livestock for the populace. I might have been raised a Quaker or a Baptist. My mind ceased to prophesize the possibilities of my fate.

The fax defined my biological homeland as a typical midwestern vicinity. Coatesville was a community that was determined to re-emerge from the barbarous ravages of nature. New Albany had its similar catastrophes, I pondered. The Tornado of 1917 shattered the northwest corner of the city. The Flood of 1937 inundated sixty-five percent of the helpless town. I remembered the horror of the 1976 twister that turned the sky green as I peered from the window of my high school English class.

My adolescent dreams of descending from prestige and wealth disappeared. It was much more likely that my birthparents emanated from a proletarian family rather than a royal one.

I sipped from a second cup of the dark roast. I glanced at my watch as the sun rose, and knew that Coatesville was three hours ahead. I wondered if my birthmother still lived in that country town. The possibility of the fact did exist. What a preposterous thought, I mused, still struggling between zeal and reason. I reminded myself of my age and almost laughed when I thought of her living in the same house for the past thirty-six years.

I stared at the telephone. Maybe the blasphemous ease of merely pushing a few touch-tones would put an end to the riddle that had tortured me for two decades. A small town that rested snugly in the heart of swaying cornfields would have Midwestern values. The ideologies of the inhabitants were certainly not like those of Southern California, in which one moves to a different dwelling an average of once every three and a half years. There must still be many American communities like Coatesville, I thought, where the townspeople are born, live, and remain until they die. My own adoptive parents, for instance, had lived in the same house on Grantline Road for over forty years.

I felt the heaviness of the receiver in my hand as I placed it against my ear. Although my grandfather was dead, my grandmother could still be living there. I dialed information.

"Operator. City, please?" echoed a faint but hurried female voice.

"Uh, Coatesville. Do you have a listing for Stewart, Otis Stewart in Coatesville?" I was completely prepared for the response, 'Sorry, sir, no listing.' I was stunned, however, by the actual reply that resounded into my ear.

"Hold for the number, please," and then a computer artificially blared a series of numerals. "The number is...7-6-4-0-8-5-2."

I grabbed a pen from a far corner on my desk.

"Repeat... 7-6-4-0-8-5-2." The audio digitized numerals bellowed, evenly spaced and without gender. I managed to scrawl the numbers onto a piece of paper and then replaced the receiver numbly. I stared at my hardly legible characters. Although Otis had passed away several years ago, there was still a telephone listing. Somebody must still live there! My grandmother? My birthmother?

I fumbled with the wrinkled paper and gaped at the seven digits for twenty minutes. Employees of the shopping center started to fill the parking places, and the rising sun reflected bright beams from the chrome bumpers. It was now eight o'clock. Gallery of Diamonds was not scheduled to open for another two hours.

I realized I was holding the combination to the ancient lock of my past--maybe a dreadful, horrible past. It had been disguised in seven simple digits. Although I was sure that many adoptees had the ability to invent illusions of grandeur about their birthmothers, I could now only recall the broken phrases from the court summary: "bad dream...cheap jewelry...too much to drink...not telling the truth."

What if I found her? The Great Search would be over. Investigating the past had become a very placid and ordinary part-time vocation in my life. The act of *finding*, on the other hand, involved swinging a machete through uncharted territory. I was terrified. I then remembered those precious moments with Carmen when I assured her that there was nothing in life to be afraid of-- the fear of storms, the fear of failure, the fear of darkness. I felt I had personally overcome all of my own fears, but then I noticed one that unrelentingly returned to torment me -- the fear of the Unknown.

The seven digits stared back at me from the wrinkled surface of business stationery. The silhouette of the diamond logo shone through from the other side. I caressed the paper, being mindful of the delicate texture between my fingers. The numbers were to my "home," in a newly defined sense. Like the numbers of one's street address or current age that is eternally memorized as a child, they would have been seven digits as deeply instilled in my brain as the date of my birth.

There was no sense in calling Mom again or Carmen either. I had to push the numbers on the telephone keypad. I dialed '1,' then the area code, then the remainder of the seven digits-- except the last one.

Then I replaced the receiver. What would I say, for heaven's sake? I tortured myself in composing my first words. What if my birthmother answered? Or my Grandmother? I began to pen a fictitious dialogue on another piece of paper. Surely the answerer would think I was a psychopath.

I was overcome by a strange, familiar, terrible feeling. I mentally returned to the day of my youth when I stood alone, freezing to death in front of that lone house on Featheringill Road. I prayed that someone would answer. Just as soon as I was acknowledged, the door was then shut again. If the lady had not let me inside her warm hearth, I surely would have died that morning in the bitter cold.

Perhaps that is what would happen all over again. I would call this number, and once the answerer heard my introduction would say, "I'm sorry, sir. You must have the wrong number. I've never heard of a Betty Price. Good-bye." Perhaps I had indeed found the door that would solve the riddle of my past. After the contents were briefly revealed, they would be resealed in a tighter defense, like a land turtle that locks itself in its shell. The pages of the past could be sucked into a Black Hole.

But I didn't die that morning on Featheringill Road, and I would be given a chance, nearly twenty years later to find out where I came from.

I re-dialed the number, including the last digit. The faint ring came from a planet outside my familiar solar system. An elderly lady answered.

"Hello?" she said.

"Hello. Is this Hattie Stewart?"

"Yes." I was thrilled and terrified on hearing the voice of another human being that shared my DNA.

"My name is Michael Watson. I'm calling you from California. Was your daughter's name Betty, who got married to a Floyd Price?" I already knew those answers, but I wanted to interject something personal, something that only a friend or relative could know, something that would arrest her attention before she slammed the receiver in my ear.

"Yes."

"Mrs. Stewart, I don't know how to tell you this, but your daughter, Betty, is my birthmother. I was adopted in 1958 after I was born in Community Hospital in Indianapolis." Although I wanted to scream that sentence, I restrained myself. Each word was paced evenly with the same volume.

"Who is this?" she asked skeptically.

I repeated my words once more.

"I'm very sorry," she said. I braced myself for what was coming next. But instead, she answered differently. "My daughter had a boy named Michael, but he was born in 1953."

"Yes, I know!" I said. "Michael David Price. I found out about him many years ago. My name happens to be Michael also, but I was named by my adoptive parents."

"Now hold on there," she continued with concern. "Betty had another child, but he was stillborn."

"I'm very sorry, Ma'am," I said apologetically. "When did that happen?"

"It was in February. In 1958."

"I'm very sorry," I repeated. Then I came to my senses. "I was born in February of 1958. That's me!" I spoke wildly. Then after using all my energy to constrain my excitement I said, "I am certainly not dead, and you are my grandmother!"

There was numbing silence. I pressed the receiver hard against my ear. Five seconds passed. I noticed I was now standing. I strained to hear. She was not speaking. Perhaps she was waiting for me to speak again. Ten seconds passed. I lost track of time. Perhaps she had been swallowed by the Black Hole. Then she spoke.

"You know," she paused, "we always wondered if you were alive."

"What do you mean, *alive*, Mrs. Stewart?" I said. "Didn't Betty, your daughter, tell you that she put me up for adoption?"

"Betty always told us that you were stillborn, but we still wondered if you were alive."

"Yes. I'm very *much* alive," I said. And before I could absorb the fact that I had gone down in the annals of the Stewart lineage as being deceased, I said, "Please tell me about Betty. I have been trying to find her since I was a teenager."

"She had a very hard life," she answered.

And then I wondered why a mother would begin a description of her own daughter in such negative terms. I would not settle for such a vague answer. Even the court summary painted a more complete picture of her.

"What does she look like, Mrs. Stewart? Where does she live?" I pleaded.

"Betty passed away thirteen years ago," she spoke regretfully.

I felt my right leg tremble. I braced myself on my desk with my free arm. "What do you mean, *she passed away?*"

"She died in 1981 in Quincy, Massachusetts. She was only forty-six. But I guess you still have uncles, aunts, and cousins here in Coatesville."

Something inside told me I should have wept. After all, my birthmother had died, and like my Grandfather Otis, seemed to die that very instant. But I didn't cry. It didn't make sense, chronologically anyway, that I was speaking to my grandmother, yet my birthmother had already passed away thirteen years ago.

"How did she die?" I asked.

"Cirrhosis of the liver."

"Did she drink?" I asked reflexively.

"Yes. She had a very hard life," she repeated.

During the next moments I explained how I derived her telephone number and gave a brief synopsis of my life, my adoptive parents, and my wife. I told her that I wanted nothing personal from her, only to know where I came from. She seemed to listen with a close ear and uttered what sounded like a closing statement, "Well, I guess I'll tell the rest of the family that they now have relatives in California."

I felt the conversation coming to an end. My birthmother was dead. Even I was dead. And now this brief and frail alien encounter would perhaps be the first and last contact with the other world. I squeezed the receiver.

"Can I call them?" I said. "I mean, don't you think they should know about me?"

"I'll let them know," she said. "I feel it would be better for me to tell the rest of the family." The conclusion of our first and possibly only interchange was nearing. I was afraid to hang up. I was enthralled to realize that I had a biological *family*, yet I was sickened to hear of my birthmother's death. My emotions were tangled. Half of my body was freezing, the other half was boiling.

I couldn't just keep the phone to my ear, I thought. I believed she was waiting for me to say goodbye first, after all, I was the one who called. "It was a pleasure talking to you, Mrs. Stewart." Although she was actually my grandmother, it would have been awkward to address her as such. "Good-bye."

"Bye, now."

The telephone was still cemented to my ear. Then before a second passed, I blurted, "Mrs. Stewart?"

"Yes." She was still there. I felt ill. Not only had I been dead for the past thirty-six years, but my birthmother had also died. I still hungered to know what she looked like. There was the possibility that Mrs. Stewart might not want to make further contact with me again. After all, I was a complete stranger, for no one in the Coatesville universe even knew of my existence.

"Mrs. Stewart," I repeated, "Why don't I send you a picture of me and my wife and my adoptive parents, and then maybe you could send me a picture of Betty and you."

"That would be fine," she answered. We exchanged addresses, bid farewell, and proceeded to hang up once again.

"Mrs. Stewart!" I cried again as I pulled the receiver back to my mouth.

"Yes."

"This might be a silly question, but what nationality are you, was Betty, am *I*? I mean, you see, I don't know who or what I am."

"Well, we're all-American," she said.

That was not the answer I expected. Mrs. Stewart did continue to explain that no one knew who my birthfather was, who apparently rendered my Mediterranean traits. "Well, I'm definitely not *all-American*," I responded, "but I'm looking forward to getting your pictures in the mail."

We bid adieu for the third time and hung up.

A lot of ground was covered during those primal moments. Hattie Stewart said her husband died in 1987. I told her I was sorry and didn't mention I learned that from a genealogical researcher. She spoke of my mother's sister and brothers--my aunt and uncles. She told me their names--Mary Jane, David, Bob. She spoke of Michael David, and another younger brother, Kenny Ray. I had another brother!

She mentioned Susie, a sister! And she spoke sadly of Debra Kay, another sibling who disappeared. She had vanished before her second birthday. Betty apparently wasn't able to provide a singular explanation, saying to some that a babysitter had stolen her and to others that a social worker had taken her.

I felt her grief as we spoke, for Debra Kay was a little girl whom everyone knew and loved, and then suddenly she disappeared from the face of the earth. I, on the other hand, was not a tragedy, but merely a child who suffered the unfortunate circumstances of being born dead.

I remember straining to hear every muttered word about the secrets of the past. Michael David was the first child born in 1953, then Debra Kay, then me, then Susie, and Kenny Ray. I had two brothers and two sisters!

The next morning I typed her a letter, trying to veil my excitement.

June 9, 1994

Dear Hattie,

It was so nice to hear your voice. I am 36 and that was the first time I have ever spoken to anyone who was a biological relative. I have searched for Betty Price since I was 17. I regret that I will never have a chance to meet her.

I am sending you a copy of the court summary that I received many years ago and a marriage license application I recently received. This is what led me to you.

I was blessed with wonderful adoptive parents who continue to live in New Albany, where I lived most of my life.

I would like to meet you one of these days and all of my relatives who would like to meet me. I am also sending pictures of my wife and me. Please send me pictures of my birthmother. I've wondered what she looked like my entire life.

Your grandson.

The following two weeks went by slowly for I had not heard another word from her. I knew that mail from Indiana to California took no more than a few days. My grandmother had professed to being eighty-four years old, and her voice lacked vitality. Perhaps she had gotten sick, or decided against mailing me any photos. Maybe she was finally at peace in knowing of my existence and decided not to let the secret venture further. Perhaps she had died.

Twice I almost called again, but now it was her turn to contact me. It was *someone's* turn to contact me, I protested to myself. After all, I was the one who had been searching for nearly twenty years. Couldn't someone just pick up the phone and call me?

The mailman came. The return address was from Coatesville. The envelope appeared scrawled over several times, with slight

The search for physical similarity. First grade photos of birthmother, Betty Stewart, the author and Michaela, the author's daughter. 1943, 1965 and 2002.

Grandfather Otis Milton Stewart. Born April 13, 1899. Died May 14, 1987. Shown at eighteen years old.

Biological grandparents. Otis and Hattie Stewart. Fiftieth wedding anniversary. April 7, 1983.

variations of my address, as if the letter was continuously returned to the sender for lack of my correct address. I opened the envelope and dove straight to the enclosed photo. It was an outdoor scene with an attractive dark-headed girl standing next to an older woman. From the date underneath the weathered polaroid, I knew the elder woman must have been my mother, and that the picture was taken just a few years before she died. I strained to see a frail resemblance of myself through the blurry snapshot. Then I realized that the younger girl was my sister, Susie. She must have been around seventeen, and for the first time I encountered a reflection of myself in the photograph of another human.

I stayed in frequent contact with my grandmother, calling her at least once a week. And, like an archeologist who carefully brushes away the dirt that conceals ancient mysteries, I probed her for more and more pieces of my past.

Mom seemed strangely calm about my discovery, and I wondered if it was because her biggest adversary had vanished. Did her sudden burst of support emerge from the fact that the unknown enemy, my birthmother, had died?

Nevertheless, I was proud of my breakthrough and made sure Mom and grandmother had each other's addresses and telephone numbers.

## 17. Two Families Become One

Labor Day was approaching. I hadn't seen my parents for many years and missed them a lot. The time seemed right to return to my childhood home. Mom said Coatesville was only three hours away by car, so I could invite Grandmother Hattie Stewart and any other birth relatives to come to New Albany. That was a brilliant idea, for if that gathering did take place, I wanted my parents to be there. I took her advice, called my grandmother, and expressed my wishes. She agreed to come "if the Good Lord was willin'."

On September 4, 1994, Carmen and I arrived in New Albany and were enjoying the relaxed pace of the small town. It was a hot Sunday, the day before Labor Day. The flight from the night before seemed long, but we were rejuvenated anticipating the new guests in the late morning.

Tires slowly crackled over the driveway's dry limestone gravel. Two cars had wheeled in front with apprehension, as when one realizes he or she might be at the wrong address. I was certain, however, who the visitors were.

I rushed outside. The next thing I remember is standing defenselessly in the center of the yard, peering into each of the car's windows. There were six passengers, four in one car and two in the other. They were also staring at me. I realized I was standing alone and felt naked. My mind was dazed, but I believe the first person out of the car was Grandmother. I recognized her from the photo she sent of her and Otis's fiftieth anniversary. She approached me with opened arms, calling me *grandson*. I hugged her reflexively.

Behind Grandmother came a younger woman with coarse, brown hair, with somewhat the same texture as my own. She lacked any trace of a smile and deliberately approached me as if I were an unknown animal species. She firmly squeezed my hands and peered deep into my eyes, studying me with scientific curiosity. The woman was Mary Jane, Aunt Mary Jane. I yearned for similarity as I beheld my birthmother's younger sister.

I was dizzily transported back to that unremembered time of my birth. The past rammed into the present. I felt I was dreaming, but the cool, refreshing grasp of her hands in the blistering September sun was real. The pages of my book of life flipped backward and forward at the speed of light. The woman's voice finally broke my semi-conscious state.

"Are you really Betty's son?" she said. I nodded.

The front yard filled with more and more people. Carmen came from behind me. Then Mom and Dad appeared and the remaining passengers. I later imagined what the neighbors thought, seeing nearly a dozen people staring at one another, standing equidistantly, as if waiting to be asked to dance.

Other than Grandmother Hattie, the guests admitted their fear of coming, since they believed the whole ordeal could have been a hoax. After Grandmother told me I wasn't supposed to be alive, I understood their feelings. I must have been like some kind of ghost.

Mom had frequent telephone exchanges with Grandmother and gave her a warm embrace like she was an old friend. Then she ushered everyone into the living room. I walked from stranger to stranger saying, "So you must be my...?" filling in the salutations with aunt, uncle, etc, while shaking their hands in a polite, businesslike manner.  During those first moments I had met two uncles, two aunts, a first cousin, and Grandmother Hattie.  Even Dad conversed with the new visitors like he had known them all his life.

"I can't believe this is real," Grandmother Hattie said. "Betty said you were stillborn."

"Michael's sure been searching for a long time." Mom said proudly, almost as if she were my professional manager.

I scanned the new faces, searching for physical similarity. I compared their eyes, noses, ears, and receding hairlines.  No one, I determined, was the spitting image of me.  The new guests later declared that none of them knew my birthfather.  And like Grandmother stated, everyone indeed looked *all-American.* There was nothing unusual or supernatural about anyone.

"Let's eat.  I'm sure you're all hungry." Mom beckoned the new guests deeper into the house.  The aroma of Mom's pot roast filled the rooms.  The kitchen table was a place I had always fondly remembered.  And now, like an unexpected fantasy, I was sitting down at that table with my parents *and* my birth family.

To my birth family, my name was Jonathan Raymond.  At least that is how Betty referred to me.  When she drank heavily, she said she had to find Jonathan Raymond, because she put him up for adoption.  When she became sober, she would refute her story, saying I was really stillborn.  But I never had a funeral, or even a memorial.  The two-sided account of my fate disturbed my family and siblings deeply. The ambience of the kitchen grew somber as we spoke about Betty, for it seemed that she indeed suffered a hard life.  She began drinking at a tender age and eventually died from the self-punishing disease only ten years older than I was currently. She had married several times, and many of her husbands were afflicted with the same obsession. It was a creepy feeling, realizing that when I was begging Judge Jameson to release the records about my birthmother, she was dying in a hospital in Quincy, Massachusetts.

I attempted to brighten the conversation, sharing the tale of the amulet I had purchased as a teenager to give Betty if I ever found her. It was almost twenty years since I had last seen it, and wherever it was I'm sure the inexpensive metal had long become green and oxidized from the dampness of my parents' house.

After finishing a cake with chocolate icing swirling my name, we returned to the living room. Uncle David, my birthmother's brother, had a surprise for me. Uncle David had prepared a home video pictorial narrated by Aunt Mary Jane. All of us crowded around Mom and Dad's old Zenith as we slid the cassette into the video player.

It began with the title, "Michael Watson--this is your life," and continued with a collage of family photos. Some were very old, with antiquated cars in the background. Some were taken during holidays, some during birthdays. The first photo was my first grade picture. Apparently, Grandmother Hattie and Mom had exchanged family memorabilia. It was a familiar photo that I hadn't seen in a long time and felt a little embarrassed viewing it once again while crowded amongst strangers. A little girl's black and white photo was adjacent to mine. She appeared to be the same age and displayed my smile and eyes. In fact, notwithstanding her opposite sex, she looked exactly like me. I smiled, thinking it must have been my sister, Susie.

Uncle David announced the child as Betty. My mother. The female who gave birth to me.

September 4, 1994. Two families unite.  L-R: Uncle Louie
Garland, Grandmother Hattie Stewart, Aunt Mary Jane Garland,
Aunt Joy Lee Stewart, the author, and Uncle David Stewart.
Photo by Carmen Watson.

1957. Biological family in
Coatesville, Indiana.
L-R: Betty, Michael David,
Grandfather Otis Stewart, Aunt
Mary Jane and Uncle Bob.
Betty is shown pregnant with
author.

It was almost too much to imagine that I entered the world through the womb of the innocent child I beheld in the television monitor. When I finally came to my senses, I wondered how many people actually possess a first grade photograph of their mother. At least one of the visitors had something to say about a particular frame, as it conjured up memories of when someone had a baby, got married, divorced, suffered a heart attack, or died. The complete Stewart lineage was on that tape. There was one photo of Grandmother Hattie as a young girl with *her* mother and family. There was also my great-great grandfather James Murphy from Blacksberry, Kentucky, posing with a large hat, double-breasted suit and a cane.

The trunks of everyone's bodies slanted forward sharply. Some neighbors had also found close seats. The reunion was equally exciting for them, for they had known my parents even before I was adopted. I don't recall the living room ever being so crowded. I sat semi-Indian style on the crammed floor with my eyes just a few feet from the screen. Carmen huddled close to me. Dad eagerly watched from his chair as he gnawed an unlit pipe.

Then there were snapshots of my siblings, Michael David, Kenny Ray, and a high school portrait of Susie. The next frame was Betty, sitting on someone's front porch with a little baby on her lap. She was quite attractive, wearing a pleasant smile, painted lips and nails, and her hair was fashionably brushed. The baby seemed to be giggling, but the cheerfulness of the room grew solemn when that frame appeared. The baby was my older sister, Debra Kay, and that had been the last photo taken of her before she had vanished. Thoughts of Debra Kay evoked sad memories. She was a little child who had yet to manifest her being. In the unrecorded annals of the Stewart genealogy, Debra Kay was a missing person.

The phone rang. Mom answered and passed it to Aunt Mary Jane. She mumbled a few words then re-passed the receiver to me. I hoisted myself from the floor, unaware that my bones weren't as flexible as in my youth. It was Michael David calling from Florida. He sounded stunned, for although I knew of him for many years, he knew nothing of me until Grandmother Hattie told him. Our dialogue was probably unlike most siblings, and more like someone had just introduced us at a party. He briefed me about his life, but remembered very little about his own mother, saying that he was raised mostly by his uncle and aunt. I told him I was glad to know that I had a brother. We exchanged telephone numbers and said goodbye.

One person looked at his watch, then the others followed suit lamentably, saying they had to drive back to Coatesville. The word goodbye was painful. I believe my own father cried. Like my inability to hang up the telephone during my first contact with Grandmother, it was difficult to accept that the people who shared my bloodline had to leave.

Although my birthmother had passed away many years before, I had finally found my long, lost family. The video was mine to keep. I would share it with my future children. On that day, in the form of magnetic tape, I possessed what millions of adoptees only dream of--their heritage.

As we bid farewell, I addressed the visitors with their new names: Uncle David, Aunt Joy Lee, Uncle Louie, Aunt Mary Jane, *another* Michael, my first cousin, and Grandmother Hattie. It had taken a little practice to form those names with my lips during our first visit, and they echoed back awkwardly into my own ears.

Carmen gathered everyone outside, and once again we were standing in the front lawn. She lined us up tightly and snapped a photograph. An amazing thing was happening, for like a bride and a groom that become one on their wedding day, two families were merging. I still had the same Mom and Dad for the past thirty-six years. That never changed. But now our family consisted of six new members. Before the visitors left, even my own Mom was addressing them with the same prefixes as I. Even though mom was only a few years younger than Hattie, she courteously called her "Grandmother" also. Before the evening ended we each had accepted our rightful position in the family hierarchy. My birth family clearly understood that Martha Watson was indeed my mother, the woman who raised and instructed me since day three of my life.

Although my birthmother had died before I met her, I received much more than I had ever asked for. I also wondered if that spectacular event of joyful fellowship could take place in another situation. Before that day there was no common denominator between our two families. Well, there was one--Michael Watson. What would happen, I marveled, if one family called upon another in which there was no previous relationship and asked to get together for a reunion? Could that be possible?

## 18. Unlocking the Door of Secrecy

Carmen and I sat silently in the airplane back to California. I always took the window side and mostly just gazed at the blanket of clouds below. Sometimes we turned to face each other, sharing a smile and a hand squeeze. The weekend had been like some kind of dream.

A fantastic joy lingered during the weeks and months that passed. Aunt Joy Lee would send letters, sometimes twice weekly, filling me in on the archives of the past while expressing the newfound happiness of my Coatesville relatives. One thing unanimously agreed upon was that the Watson-Stewart Reunion was the event of the century.

Months later I continued to share my success story with every person I met. I had yet to meet my siblings, but had received weekly mail from my *new* aunts and grandmother. Each letter slowly filled in the missing blanks about the life of Betty.

Shortly afterwards, Dad died. My birth family that I met only months earlier had returned once again. I was overjoyed that they had the chance to meet Dad. The joy of finding my biological family was in direct proportion to the agony of losing Dad. Although grief-stricken, I still maintained the belief that everything in life was good and felt that the laws of the universe had somehow intervened once again. Like the poppy that briefly emerges in the spring and washes away after the first rain, a new family had been born. There was, I realized, always pain that was associated with birth. The difference was the chronological order.

There was never a practical or legal use for my unamended birth certificate. Nevertheless, I always felt it was rightly mine. And even though I had lost the only father I had known, I still wondered if the name of my birthfather would be revealed.

I re-submitted a request to the Indiana Adoption History division, giving Betty's maiden name. I obeyed the Indiana State Board of Health's recorded telephone directions and enclosed a copy of my drivers license with the correct fee.

My reply:

> A registration form must be completed by a birthparent
> <u>and</u> the adoptee to meet the criteria for a match. We can
> only release your original birth record when we have <u>both</u>
> consents on file.

I resent the request stating my birthmother had died thirteen years ago.

My second reply:

> We are in receipt of an Indiana Adoption History
> registration form; however, this cannot be filled... We need a
> copy of the death certificate for Betty Price.

Reading that letter offended me, because I had to show proof that my birthmother had died before I could receive proof that I was born. It appeared that the State of Indiana had squeezed the choices of obtaining my original birth certificate to a mere two: first, my birthmother would have to die; second, I would have to prove it.

The next week I acquired a copy of Betty's death certificate. It was the first one I had ever seen and it was quite strange that it belonged to the birthmother I had never met. The document was neatly typed and titled, The Commonwealth of Massachusetts, standard certificate of death. It stated her address, recorded her occupation as homemaker, and listed her age at forty-six. Further down it stated the name of the cemetery where she was buried. The field for cause of death seemed hurriedly scrawled, saying *Hepatic encephalopathy*, due to a consequence of *Gram negative septicemia*. In layman's terms, Betty Price died from alcohol destruction of her liver and brain.

I sent a duplicate request to the Indiana State Department of Health (ISDH), but this time with a copy of the death certificate. Shortly thereafter I received this letter:

> The consents have been filed in the office of the State Registrar of Vital Records and a written confirmation of the continued desire to participate in the release of information has been received from the registrants. A copy of the Record of Adoption and Certificate of Birth were released on this date to Mr. Michael C. Watson (Adult Adoptee).
>
> Any office or agency holding files pertaining to this proceeding is authorized to release identifying and/or non-identifying information to Mr. Michael C. Watson only upon receipt of his request and proper identification.

The ISDH then sent what I had requested for most of my life. Although a photocopy, it was official and bore the raised seal of Indiana. It was titled *Certificate of Live Birth*, and specified data that was always familiar to me. Under the large space given for the first, middle, and last name of father was center-spaced and typed *unknown*. At the bottom was the signature of Dr. William Fitzgerald. There was another blank in which the doctor appeared to have made a mistake, blacking out the "yes" answer to Legitimate?, rechecking the box "no".

My last name was Price. The typed words dedicated to my first and middle name was not Jonathan Raymond, as my birth relatives mentioned, but was instead the single word--"infant." Other than in her imagination, it seemed that Betty had never named me.

When Betty was dismissed from the hospital on that cold February morning of 1958, she left without me. When she died, her reason for relinquishing me died with her. Whatever hurdle was set before me, I have been thankful to live the life of an adoptee. I am also thankful that my adoptive parents loved me, giving me immense purpose. I was disconcerted, however, that I had entered the world without a name.

Enclosed with the copy of the birth certificate were three familiar papers; the *Decree, the Petition for Custody of Child* and the *Order*. The probate court had kept that information in a secret folder for many years. Glancing at one document again, I read something I didn't remember: "The court further finds the prayer of said petitioners should be granted and adoption should be made as prayed for by the petitioners." There was never a prayer granted for Betty, however.

There was a new document entitled, *Affidavit and Consent for Adoption*, dated one day after my birth. The single page specified Betty Price as my natural mother, that she felt it was in my best interest to be adopted by Stoy and Martha Watson, and that she had made this decision on her own free will.

Then I saw Betty's signature written on the same form with my name and my parents, as if this mutual decision were made by everyone, including me. For a fleeting moment, I wondered what must have gone through her mind when the pen was in her hand.

Two decades of wonderment have naturally instilled me with a never-ending curiosity. Therefore, this book could never succinctly end. As I neared the age of forty, I finally met my birth brothers, Kenny Ray and Michael David in 1994 and my sister Susie in 1995. However, it seems that the conclusion of my journey has led me to the beginning of yet another--the search for my missing sister, Debra Kay.

The only state record that exists for Debra Kay is her birth certificate. There is no evidence that she was ever adopted in the state of Indiana or that she was living in a foster home. Inharmonious with Betty's story, there was never a police or sheriff's report that she was kidnapped by a babysitter, social worker, or that she was even missing at all. Other possibilities exist; she was perhaps adopted in another state or simply given away.

If she was relinquished to an unknown family, many of these children were given a *delayed certificate of birth* requested by the new parents. In the case of Debra Kay, she would be living in a surreal world with a new name, birth date, and more unaware of her creation than I was.

All evidence of my sister, Debra Kay, has vanished. As of the publication of this book, Debra Kay is a missing person. If the reader happens to know any information, please contact the publisher.

I witnessed the birth of my beautiful first child, Michaela. I can still recall her first human cry that broke forth from nine months of silence. Whenever I look into her eyes, I see the sum total of my being; every element that formed me. For the non-adoptee, this may seem unimportant. For me, it is a wonderful miracle. I suppose the one who most appreciates the sunrise is the one who has tasted the dark. Michaela will always know her Mom and Dad. By reviewing the pages of her baby book, she will discern her cosmic coordinates and how she originated on our earth.

My ancient voyage has bestowed many truths that have made life more beautiful. I offer them here for adoptees and nonadoptees who desire more meaning in their lives. Carry them on your journeys and you will have tremendous purpose and accomplish amazing things:

> Love others *and* yourself.
> Do even the smallest of things with passion and love.
> Follow your spark.
> Use your talents.
> Say with belief: "I can do that!"
> Search for God inside yourself, and you will see God in everything else.

ADULT ADOPTEE RIGHTS POSITION STATEMENT OF THE

AMERICAN ADOPTION CONGRESS LEGISLATIVE COMMITTEE

All adopted adults have the right to know their original identities and their medical and ancestral histories. In addition, they have the right to associate freely with others, including biological relatives, without government restriction. In most states these rights are violated by restrictive laws, court decisions, the practice of some adoption attorneys and adoption professionals, and public and private agency policy and practice.

It is critical to educate the public about the rights of adult adoptees and to restore these rights in law. To these ends, the AAC Legislative Committee stands ready to consult and work with organizations, legislators, agencies and individuals to re-establish adult adoptees' rights so that all adults shall be treated equally under the law.

# *PART TWO*

# *A  Legendary*

# *Contest of Love*

*Martha Velia Watson today.*

# In Honor of All Moms

In 1993, at a time when I was still searching for my birthmother, I started a mother's appreciation contest. Although adopted into a family of very loving parents, I was always curious to know about the woman who gave birth to me. The contest would be in honor of my adoptive mother and my birthmother. It would also give kids a chance to express their appreciation for their own moms. I called a few schools and invited students to write an essay about *Why Mom Deserves a Diamond*™. The most creative and sincere contestant would receive a quarter-carat diamond now valued at five hundred dollars.

I received over two hundred entries from students who poetically illustrated why their moms should merit the gem. It was fascinating how students expressed their appreciation for the women who gave birth to them, and I could relate to most of their writings as if they were speaking about my own adoptive mother.

Reviewing each labor of love gave me a feeling of wholeness that was indescribable. With vibrant imagination, these young adults approached the voluntary writing assignment as a once-in-a-lifetime chance to honor their mothers. I soon realized that it was the wonderful memories of our mothers that brought forth the most creative expressions of love, and our mothers are almost always the common denominator of our hearts.

On Mother's Day, I named sophomore Margaret Ketchersid as our first-place Diamond Winner. It was a quiet, yet heartwarming ceremony as Margaret presented the diamond to her mother, Ruth. Afterwards, I re-read that mound of essays and selected fifty additional *second-place winners*, choosing to award them a beautiful African red garnet. The next day, I invited the garnet winners to claim their prize. It was a wonderful feeling to hear those kids recite their words of love.

The following year, entries bombarded the store by the hundreds. By the deadline, the gentle hill of entries on my desk had exploded into a mountain. One submission moved me completely, and one grand prizewinner received a diamond while two hundred additional kids were awarded semi precious gems. I believe I was fortunate in meeting every winner.

What began as nothing more than a humble tribute for my own mother evolved into a type of ministry in which thousands of kids are recognized for their achievements while becoming a little closer to their moms.

The *Why Mom Deserves a Diamond*™ contest has since sprouted wings, reaching every state in the nation. Over twenty thousand letters are mailed to Gallery of Diamonds annually. The contest has benefited everyone it has touched, and has been instrumental in giving kids a higher self-esteem. It has become symbolic as an exercise in love, and I am quite sure the thought process involved for every writer instills a moral to appreciate one's own parents, whether adoptive or not, and *especially while they are living.*

## Love

If there is anything *real* in this world, I'm convinced it is a universal power called love. Whether it is born from our hearts or from a Divine Mind, I have seen it cross every border of culture and religion. I have heard thousands of kids from every socio-economic background recite their poetic expressions to their moms. When words are written, thoughts and feelings are reinforced; when words come forth from the lips, they become *real*.

Perhaps the love of parents for their children is the strongest human feeling. I am grateful that I was first loved by my adoptive parents. Like learning all things from our parents, I learned love. It is easy for me to see love in all things. Like the fundamental forces of nature, it is a power I recognize that holds the universe together in wondrous balance.

**1993.**

*First Diamond Winner
Margaret Ketchersid
presents the precious gem
to her mother, Ruth.*

# Past Diamond Winners

The following is a compilation of Diamond Winners since 1993. On Diamond Day, each winner is awarded a diamond to give to their mom.

## 1993

Her love is not blind

It is clear and forgiving

Her touch is all-knowing

Her joy is life giving

This angel, my mother, gives of herself

And illuminates me

With compassion's true wealth

A symbol of courage

And  strength she remains

And understands all my joys and pains

To gaze at my mother

Who strives beyond duty

Is to see radiate

Her unique warming beauty!

The sweet voice of mother

Her strong, safe, embrace

I long to possess

Her pure, natural, grace

My Mother, my guide

And gemstone so rare

Deserves out of likeness

A diamond as fair

**Margaret Ketchersid, Grade 10**

**Huntington Beach, CA**

## 1994

No one knows what it's like

To walk in her shoes

When every game she played with me

She always seemed to lose

And the note from Santa Claus

Seemed to look the same

As the writing on the lunchbags

Where she wrote my name

In all the falls I took

And the cuts I made

She fixed me up with only a

Kiss and a purple band-aid

But of all the things she ever said

And all the nights sleeping in my bed

I promised I'd give her

The diamonds in the sky

When all she said she ever wanted

Were the diamonds in my eyes

**Alison Murphy, Grade 10**

**Mission Viejo, CA**

## 1995

Whether I stand on land or shore

I know I couldn't love my mother more

Always caring, always there

In times that are good. In times of despair

Magical lands we like to explore

When she reads aloud

From classical lore I thank you, Mom, at each

day's end. You really are my best friend

**Scott Kircher, Grade: 6**

**Corona del Mar, CA**

## 1996

Shadows flickering, dancing about. Even the moon is terrified. I lie wide awake, petrified as the distant Silhouettes come dancing towards me. Then suddenly they disappear . As she flicks on the light. Her soothing smile, her comforting voice. And the monsters are all gone.

**Lauren Kiang, Grade: 7**

**Mission Viejo, CA**

## 1996

Million gallons of love, two pinches of creativity, twelve cups of niceness, two gallons of understanding. Million drops of unique and beautifulness, any other items that might make your mother wonderful. Mix well, bake two seconds. I guarantee my mother!

**Megan Darakjian, Grade: 4**

**Mission Viejo, CA**

## 1997

Burning sands, ever shifting

Desert of life I must pass through

When I sink, two hands are lifting

Helping me to start anew

She's the oasis where I may rest

She, who always knows me best

Diamond in the rough

**Genevieve Slunka, Grade: 11**

**Irvine, CA**

## 1997

My mom is a cozy place

Like a warm cup of cocoa

Or a pillow trimmed with lace

My Mom's love is all mine

I can always depend

She's more than a mom

She's my best friend

**Jessica Barraco, Grade: 4**

**Irvine, CA**

## 1998

Her lips are roses, her complexion is cream. She understands my deepest thoughts and dreams. She is my angel with a halo of gold. She is my mother.

**Tawyna Ravy, Grade: 7**

**Yorba Linda, CA**

## 1998

A heavenly calm, and pure state of grace. A lovely expression falls on her face. A whisper of words, like velvety lace. Soft summer's glow, in securing embrace. My Mother.

**Jennifer Planenhorn, Grade: 8**

**Valencia, CA**

## 1998

My mother deserves a diamond because she's unique, priceless, perfect, pure, precious, dazzling, flawless and rare. She sparkles with love and glistens with knowledge. She is a gem to me.

**Vicki Ann Blood, Grade: 4**

**Lakewood, CA**

## 1998

A diamond has all the colors of the rainbow. My mom deserves a diamond because she is all the colors in my life.

**Jason Kirstein, Grade: 3**

**Irvine, CA**

## 1999

The salt of my life is my mom, which gives taste in all the recipes of life. She is the ingredient that gives inspiration in my journey to my goals.

**Roberto Ruiz, Grade 5**

**Los Angeles, CA**

## 1999

Gem of my heart, fair as can be. A star from heaven brought to earth. A precious jewel beyond compare. Deserving this diamond is my angel, my mother.

**Chris Olsen-Phillips, Grade 6**

**Bloomington, IN**

## 1999

My mother has a heart of gold. Her love is the most precious thing I hold. And when I look at her I see. An angel sent to protect me.

**Brice Tomlinson, Grade 6**

**Addison, TX**

## 1999

A rose, pure and true. Movements of a rainbow. Voice like silk, and laughter like the drumming of raindrops. Diamond of life. Sparkling and glittering with unimaginable beauty. My mother.

**Paula Kim, Grade 7**

**Mission Viejo, CA**

## 1999

Her touch- like breezes on a warm summer day. Her laugh- like one million tears being dried away. Mom is her name for which there is no other. Mom- mine forever.

**Blair Perkins, Grade 5**

**Orange, CA**

*2000*

Her hair like the swaying sea cradling a sunset. Eyes like two blue sparkling sapphires. Hands as smooth as gold silk. A voice soft like the gentle wind. Mom.

**Sandy Enriquez, Grade: 5**

**Garden Grove, CA**

*2000*

The soothing sound of her voice melts away my sorrow. The gentleness of her touch relieves my deepest pains. The warmth of her sparkling eyes penetrates my soul. Mom.

**Rachel Tomberlin, Grade: 7**

**Apple Valley, CA**

*2000*

A glorious angel sent from heaven, with beauty like a dove. Her voice drains all sadness. A brilliant star shining through the darkness. My friend, my mom.

**Jennifer Scruggs, Grade: 5**

**Amarillo, TX**

*2000*

A vast lake sparkling with sunlight. A pure meadow with the gentlest breeze. My mother is more beautiful than all of these. My angel. My mother.

**Victor Taylor, Grade: 5**

**New Albany, IN**

*2000*

A flower that blossoms everyday

A stream that always flows

An adventure that has just begun

A book that never ends

A candle that will never die. Mother.

**Tiffany Lamanski, Grade: 7**

**Buena Park, CA**

*2000*

My mother's love is like a blanket, shielding me from cold winds of harm. Embraced within her soft touch, I am safe. Sacrificing all, she comforts me forever.

**Laura Cataldi, Grade: 10**

**Buffalo, NY**

*2000*

My mother is an angel. This is true, I know. She's an everlasting hug, that'll never let me go. Knowing that I'm loved, because she told me so.

**Ashley Goodell, Grade: 8**

**Okemos, MI**

*2000*

She is like a wave. As tribulations appear in my life, the tide rises and she flows to my side. Her flowing nature calms my storm. Mom, my refuge.

**Ashley Kreidler, Grade: 11**

**Delphos, OH**

## 2001

Mom is a masterpiece created with love. Her sparkling smile shines from above. Bountiful in kindness she proceeds with great care. Without knowing how much I appreciate her there.

**Alyssa Connella, Grade: 7**

**Mission Viejo, CA**

## 2001

Behold the ark that bears the covenant of conception. From her womb the living bond arose. And so it is I must behold, my mother, the temple of creation.

**Jesus Hernandez, Jr., Grade: 12**

**Houston, TX**

## 2001

A beautiful rose that blooms in July. With bright golden sapphires - those are her eyes. Her hair is black, like the calm, silent night. That's my mom all right!

**E.J. Debowski, Grade: 4**

**Laguna Niguel, CA**

## 2002

My beautiful rose is fresh from the garden. Her eyes sparkle like the dew on the soft petals. Her smile glistens like a rainbow. She is my charming mother.

**Harry Hudson, Grade: 2**

**Mission Viejo, CA**

## 2002

She is a saint, whose love is great Giving of herself, she knows not hate Kind her eyes, and soft her touch Because of her, I have so much.

**Matthew Scott, Grade: 11**

**Belton, MO**

## 2002

My mother is a river meandering in and out, flowing into every part of my life. Her banks overflow with love, kindness, gentleness and patience.

**Amanda Wheeler  Grade: 7**

**Mission Viejo, CA**

## 2003

Essence of happiness in this gray world. She taught me to respect life, while leaving my footprint. But in comparison, mine are as oarstrokes upon the water.

**Logan Cluttey., Grade: 8.**

**Rancho Santa Margarita, CA**

## 2003

My mother - a rock, silent and firm. My mother - a river, peaceful and calm. Mother - the Sun, warm and loving. She is the greatest wonder of creation.

**Travis Dziad, Grade: 6.**

**Greenville, SC**

## 2003

My Mom is like jewels glimmering through the night sky. Her eyes sparkle like rain dropping from the clouds. I love you mom, all the time.

**Aris Simsarian. Grade: 2.**

**Mission Viejo, CA**

## 2004

My mother's blue eyes are magical fountains in heaven. Her voice calls upon the angels to sing. The sunset is a sign that she is in my heart.

**Tyler Buttle  Grade: 5**

**Mission Viejo, CA**

## 2004

Eyes sparkling, like iridescent drops of rain. Smiles warm, as hot cocoa on frigid rosebud lips. Loving, deeper than all the oceans and seas. Mother...my sanctuary.

**Lindsey Croft  Grade: 12**

**Grass Valley, CA**

## 2004

Her voice- a chorus of angels. Her kisses- a butterfly's whisper. Her spirit- a gentle summer breeze. Her love- a deep sea. My mother... a precious diamond.

**Erica Haggerty  Grade: 7**

**Brea, CA**

### Treasured Writings of the Past

Since 1993, over 140,000 kids have submitted words of love in the Why Mom Deserves a Diamond™ contest. Following are some of the most cherished writings. The author hopes the following letters of love will instill a moral in all to understand more fully the value of mom in our lives.

Brielle Saracini wrote the following poem for her mom, Ellen, in memory of her father, Victor Saracini. Brielle's father was the pilot of the plane that crashed into the South Tower of the World Trade Center on September 11, 2001. Brielle has been presented with the first Honorable Mention Award of a Mother's Crown diamond and garnet necklace. Her poem represents the courage of every mom in our nation.

*Mom deserves diamonds*

*She does everyday*

*Mom stands strong*

*Although dad's far away*

*Missing her husband*

*Cause dad left on 9/11*

*Now her heart lies within heaven*

**Brielle Saracini. Grade: 7**

**Yardley, PA**

## By State

## Arizona

A beacon in the storm. She shines brightly lighting my path. Away from harm, leading me towards calm waters into her peaceful embrace.

**Robert Gibbons, Grade: 11**

**Phoenix, AZ**

## California

You are the soothing, but sudden sea. You are the graceful, but twirling carousel. You are the elegant, but watchful swan. And you are forever a diamond in my heart.

**Tiffany Allen. Grade: 8**

**Glendale, CA**

As the lotus yearns to awaken in the sweet morning light, my mother's undying love is seeping through the cracks of the earth, filling the world with happiness.

**Sneha Antani. Grade: 9**

**Anaheim, CA**

She is my stem. She is my sun locked in my heart. In sunlight of bloom. The touch of silk. The smell of a rose. Always my mom.

**Karena Arreola. Grade: 5**

**Garden Grove**

A gentle summer's breeze, a soft moonlit night. The scent of dew in the morning and tranquil showers. All are nature's perfection. Yet none can compare to my mother.

**Michael Baello, Grade: 9**

**Anaheim, CA**

Dear Mother, The wounds I felt were healed by you. The paths unknown you guided me through. From the beginning of time, and towards the end, I've finally realized that you're my best friend.

**Nghiem Banh, Grade: 10**

**Santa Ana, CA**

Her funny, quiet ways have left more than footprints on my heart, they've left a curving, two-lane highway that yawns through the beautiful orange summer trees.

**Katie Bruce, Grade: 12**

**Grass Valley, CA**

She'll comfort all my pains. Like the winds calm the rains. And I'd bring her countless dishes. Overflown with jeweled riches. Reaching high past her courage to the mountains.

**Glenda Cea, Grade: 7**

**Pasadena, CA**

"Diamonds are forever" trill silhouettes, but I know better. Diamonds are cool hands on fevered brows. Diamonds are bedtime kisses banishing monsters. Diamonds are my mother's eyes, forever.

**Kathleen Choi, Grade: 11**

**Fountain Valley, CA**

My mom is like a sheet of music that guides me through my songs. Like a compass that guides me through the forest. She guides me through life.

**Richard Cinco, Grade: 4**

**Foothill Ranch, CA**

My mom taught me to use the wings we made together. Soaring, she's the beacon guiding me, the person in the clouds waiting for me to come home.

**Robert Crabbs, Grade: 10**

**San Juan Capistrano, CA**

My mother, roses in the springtime. Sun beams dappling the frolicsome waves, cascading waterfalls of love. Mists of laughter. Rainbows of never ending friendship.

**Lauren Cruz, Grade: 6**

**Orange, CA**

There's no one in the world like my mother. I breathe her in so deep. When she holds me in her arms her soft brown hair and sparkling eyes always make me smile. I love her so with all my heart. I hope we will never be apart.

**Michael Cumpian, Grade: 7**

**Santa Ana, CA**

Her voice, like a soft sleep-song from the heavens. Her touch, like a kiss from an angel. Her eyes like a diamond twinkling above. She is my mother.

**R. Adam Diaz, Grade: 5**

**Garden Grove, CA**

Something about you, mom, seems so natural and complete. Like we were meant to be together and nothing could ever change the way I feel about you. Maybe it's how our love and emotions complement each other so well. Or maybe it's that we dream the same dreams. Whatever it is, it grows stronger and deeper everyday.

**John Dinh, Grade: 11**

**Fountain Valley, CA**

Time has passed, blown by winds. Of life, of love, of feeling. But through it all it stands alone- remains forever, eternal. What we have cannot be matched, replaced, or ever altered. Through all the changes made of us. Our love will never fail.

**April Evans, Grade: 9**

**Santa Ana, CA**

My mom's love is never ending, it shows so much it blinds me. When I am with her I feel like I can do impossible things.

**Dante Ferri, Grade: 6**

**Lake Forest, CA**

My mom, a daisy in a pasture of galloping winds. My mom, a glistening tear streaming down my cheek. My mom, the heart of the world.

**Jennifer Hagen, Grade: 5**

**Coto De Caza, CA**

The jeweler etches a magical work of art. Tools of love, compassion. Virtues, so it won't fall apart. Jeweler smiles, knowing it's none other. The diamond is my mother.

**Dominique Hilsabeck, Grade: 12**

**Huntington Beach, CA**

Lonely cries and innocent prayers. Rockingchair lullabies and heartbroken tears. Your love makes my very being melt with the sun, rivers, heaven, time. You are my eternity.

**Becky Hindt, Grade: 12**

**Smartville, CA**

Mom you're everything. Through time, you made me see, just what life is meant to be. Through hugs, my tears vanish. And laughter mends my broken dreams.

**Lauren Hopkins, Grade: 8**

**Lake Forest, CA**

My mother has a beauty that goes beyond the skin. She is a tower of strength that stands bravely through the storm, and emerges stronger yet with a shining smile.

**Jessica Hulce, Grade: 8**

**San Clemente, CA**

A pearl amongst oysters. A smile amongst frowns. She is grace and beauty personified. A diamond lasts forever. And so does her splendor.

**Megan Hutchinson, Grade: 10**

**Laguna Niguel, CA**

I have a special mom this you'll see. She is the moon and I am the star. Teaching me so when I'm an adult I will go far. She is the roots and I am the tree. Teaching important things to me. I love you!

**Alissa Isenberg, Grade: 4**

**Laguna Niguel, CA**

Like crystal waters, her wisdom flows. Like the mighty sun, her kindness glows. Like the frosty moonbeams, her love is forever.

**Alyssa Jordan, Grade: 7**

**Irvine, CA**

The boundless sky above and its majestic entity. Your love reaches far beyond. The love you have for me in two different worlds. Miles apart we stand. But one day streets of gold will guide our feet and I will be led by your hand.

**Ann Kang, Grade: 11**

**Irvine, CA**

She's my heart. She's my soul. She's the one who makes me whole. She's my spirit with pride and desire. She's the water that calms my fire. She's my Mother.

**Albert Kazi, Grade: 6**

**Santa Ana, CA**

We all know diamonds are bright. But with my mom's heart, our home becomes light. Setting example by loving, caring without rest. Love tells me my mom is the best.

**Timmy Kelemen, Grade: 6**

**Artesia, CA**

Gazing at such beauty. Such aesthetic elegance. My thoughts drift to songs of a robin. Such wondrous cadence. As perfect as a rose. So soft, so gentle, so sweet. My mom is most deserving. For she is in each heartbeat.

**Priya Khanijou, Grade: 11**

**Irvine, CA**

Mom deserves a diamond. She's the heart of my life. The extra spark in me. My life support. The many facets of her life. But still finds times for me.

**Jeff Lai, Grade: 5**

**Orange, CA**

I am adopted. Though I have never met my birthmother, I think she was very sad when she gave me up for adoption. She was very courageous. My adoptive mom is super. She has a good imagination and does a great job taking care of me. I think both deserve love.

**Jackie Kuhns, Grade: 4**

**Irvine, CA**

My mom is my living treasure. I admire her precious smile and her understanding soul. Her heart is filled with extreme beauty and wonder. No wonder I love her so!

**Yuri Lara, Grade: 8**

**Santa Ana, CA**

My mom is the sun after a rain of tears. She is the drain of all my cries and fears. She is the fire that keeps me alive.

**Adrianna Martinez, Grade: 7**

**Laguna Hills, CA**

Skin as soft as angel's wings. All her joy from simple things. Eyes of sapphire, heart of gold. Only a diamond could complete this mold.

**Katie Merrill, Grade: 6**

**Westminster,CA**

She is an unmmoving mountain, yet a free-flying bird. An unbeakable boulder, yet a fragile porcelain doll. The wind in my hair, and the blanket protecting me.

**Ryan Moore, Grade: 8**

**Mission Viejo, CA**

A diamond and my mother
Are two of the same
Diamonds all around her
Sparkle in her name
For never has there been
A dark and starless night
For with the shining of my mother's eyes
From darkness comes light
Dew on morning rose, diamonds in the sky
Kind words when a new day starts
All these things I see in her--
The diamond of my heart

**Lauren O' Hara, Grade: 9**

**Irvine, CA**

You filled my days with rainbow lights, fairytales and sweet dream nights. A kiss to wipe away my fears. Gingerbread to ease my fears.

**Rashika Patel, Grade: 8**

**Orange, CA**

My mother's hands are soft and warm. They comfort and hold me tight. They hold the light that guides me home, and calm me late at night.

**Janelle Patterson, Grade: 8**

**Yorba Linda, CA**

In the safety of her womb I once hid. We were of one flesh. She was my substance. I entered the world through her scared and alone. But she comforted me. Through the years I grew in her likeness. For every bump, cut or bruise there were kisses and kind words that would gently wash over me and soothe my pain.

**Julia Koller-Nielson, Grade: 9**

**Fountain Valley, CA**

Use fine wood, make it splinter free. Carve a face that's full of glee. Make lips to kiss and arms to hug. Make her perfect, not a kink or bug. Then finally add a heart with love.

**Laura Poladian, Grade: 4**

**Fullerton, CA**

A glittering glow, shining so bright-- a silkiness softness, touching my heart-- reflecting love through a phantom of colors--caring and glistening--sharing and listening--my lovely mother.

**Rio Ponce, Grade: 5**

**Huntington Beach, CA**

Any woman can bear a child, which is no amazing feat; but raising a son or daughter makes the word "mother" complete; and beyond the call of duty, my mother does ascend; not only does she help me grow, she also is my friend.

**Jennifer Reed, Grade: 12**

**Huntington Beach, CA**

She is like a stone in the middle of a river that causes the water to alter it's course. She is like a light constantly pointing me in the right direction. A rope that binds me to my family.

**Diana Relth, Grade: 4**

**Irvine, CA**

They walked out, you walked in. More than a mom, more like a friend. Needed a hand, I got two. Prayed for an angel, God sent you.

**Katie Ruffalo, Grade: 8**

**Trabuco Canyon, CA**

You are wings, guiding my broken flight. You are a beacon, leading me through storms. You take my weaknesses and make me strong. I love you mom.

**Ryan Russell, Grade: 8**

**Lake Forest, CA**

I want to soar to my mom's heart flower, and make a honeycomb gift of love. Someday my mom will clasp the whole world in her hands.

**Eric Rygh, Grade: 1**

**Brea, CA**

Waves break gently on a distant shore. Tree leaves fall until there's no more. At dawn birds sing in lush trees. Mother's voice, a cool soft breeze.

**Caitlin Schafer, Grade: 7**

**Mission Viejo, CA**

Warm caramel Sundays, afternoon giggles and evening tears, stormy eyes and an Irish heart. My link to the past, my path to the future. My best friend...my mother.

**Erin Swanson, Grade: 9**

**Santa Ana, CA**

Together on the Sea of Life. She, my teacher. I, her pupil. The Seasons change. Through coolness of fall. The mistakes through harshness of winter. The forgiveness through newness of spring. The memories through dryness of summer. She, my creator. I, her immortality.

**Momo Takahashi, Grade: 10**

**Mission Viejo, CA**

As though you see the dawn - the sun rising into the sky becomes ashamed. A mother is graceful, beauty in her ways that the sun is not capable of creating.

**Carly Thomas, Grade: 7**

**Woodland Hills, CA**

My mother painted my face, chiseled my thoughts and carved my path towards success. I owe her much but can only repay this artist with the love within my heart.

**My Truong, Grade: 8**

**Long Beach, CA**

My mother's the moon that shines on my face when I sleep. She's the sun that strengthens my heart deep. She's the eternal diamond of my soul.

**MichelleVu, Grade: 8**

**Huntington Beach, CA**

Shadows of time fall gently across her perfect face. Laughlines sweetly take their place with each smile that she gives. Mother...softly being pulled into yet another decade of life.

**Khadija Yakub, Grade: 8**

**Garden Grove, CA**

My mother of eternal youth and joy. Who loves flowers and birds and all of nature's creatures. Loves me the best: stirring hope, teaching life. She is my true companion.

**LilyYang, Grade: 7**

**Mission Viejo, CA**

## Colorado

My mother's eyes sparkle like irridescent dew free-falling from a tall palace. Her heart shines as an enslaved bird who had recently been freed. She is spectacular.

**Connor Bryan, Grade: 6**

**Colorado Springs, CO**

My mother's radiant beauty resembles the silver moon lighting up the night. Guiding her precious children through the unsteady stream of life, she stands strong with dignity.

**Nikki Hernandez, Grade: 6**

**Englewood, CO**

Her eyes a thick forest of trees, all knowing and all seeing. Her face smooth and milk white. She is an essence of all things beautiful.

**Richard Miller, Grade: 6**

**Colorado Springs, CO**

## Florida

Always there to walk beside me. My mom is an angel from above. A beautiful rainbow through clouds so stormy, she glows with remarkable love.

**Meredith Rogerson, Grade: 8**

**Boca Raton, FL**

## Indiana

My mother, a calm, steady fountain of wisdom. My mother, the driving force that unites our family. My mother, a glittering diamond in a world of darkness.

**Sarah Abraham, Grade: 8**

**Indianapolis, IN**

My mom is like a raindrop. She transforms my life anew. Like rain nourishes a flower, she helps me blossom into the person I will become.

**Katie Hensel, Grade: 8**

**Indianapolis, IN**

A quiet and peaceful beach and suddenly, the storm of life starts to shake me. I cry out for help. Quickly and caringly she comes to me. My mother.

**Ruth Ringenberg, Grade: 10**

**South Bend, IN**

Not even the diamond flare on winter snow, the sapphire sparkle in the heaven's glow, or the moonstone shimmer in the stars above can compare to her undying love.

**Jessica Schultz, Grade: 8**

**Fort Wayne, IN**

My mother is a forest. Many flowers, many trees. Cutting through the middle is a path that twists and weaves. Guiding me through my life. Mother, sister, daughter, wife.

**Sammi Smith, Grade: 6**

**Granger, IN**

## Illinois

My mother. .splashing all of her warm love. Shedding her love like glistening beams of warm sunlight, her love streams into me like an explosion of shimmering fireworks. Mother.

**Kalynn Fowler, Grade:5**

**Chicago, IL**

## Kansas

My mom, a rose in bloom. Her presence makes the world a sweeter place. Giving me strength to fly. But providing a sturdy branch to land on.

**Regan Doyle, Grade: 10**

**Overland Park, KS**

My mom, like a lighthouse, skims her light over my wandering ship, guiding me back to the safe and warm brightness of her forever gleaming glow.

**Catherine Lillard, Grade: 10**

**Overland Park, KS**

A diamond is forever...maybe so. Mom, you are forever, always through my heart, through my mind. Through your hands, that carved lives. For generations to come.

**Joshua Shipley, Grade: 12**

**Overland Park, KS**

## Kentucky

Like branches on a tree, Mother's love grows in different directions. Extremely loving and truthful. Even though our branches grow separate ways, our roots remain as one.

**Justin Bareis, Grade: 8**

**Louisville, KY**

## Louisiana

My mother is the light in the darkness. Her glow never dies. She is always helping others find their way. She guides me.

**Erin Classen, Grade: 7**

**Metaire, LA**

## Massachusetts

Mom- like the morning sun. Always shimmering and bringing warmth to all. Mom- a bear full of power and might, always protective and caring.

**Paul Brown, Grade: 6**

**Dracut, MA**

## Michigan

Her eyes like sapphires...bright, yet soft as the morning light. She brings such joy to my soul. Without her, my life wouldn't be whole.

**Cortneee Schlabach, Grade: 8**

**Sturgis, MI**

As I walk through the dark corridors of my troubles and through the labyrinth of my life, my mother holds the lantern to show me the way.

**Niranjan Ramadas, Grade: 8**

**Troy, MI**

Mom's love reaches past all obstacles, like the warmth of radiant sunlight extends over all the earth. She is the sun breaking through my shadows.

**KatieTruesdell , Grade: 11**

**Schoolcraft, MI**

## Missouri

When my family was homeless, my mom took care of us. She would tuck my sister and I in the van at night and read us stories.

**Name Withheld, Grade: 3**

**O'Fallon, MO**

## New Jersey

A heart of gold shining diamond eyes, My hand she holds, singing lullabies. Silvery raindrops of calmness glimmering in her serene face. Her radiant smile filled with warmness-- a reflection of love and grace.

**Emily Looney, Grade: 6**

**Lawrenceville, NJ**

## New York

Like the Statue of Liberty; proud and strong. Scintillating beauty, guiding me with light, my mother is the anchor to the new world in front of me.

**Dawn Glaves, Grade: 9**

**East Northport, NY**

None deserving of the glittering gem than my mother. A rose, she blossoms hope, inspiration, and love. Joyfully, she sparkles, the diamond of my life.

**Kelly Mc Lachlan, Grade: 10**

**E. Amherst, NY**

A waterfall picture perfect. A glorious stream flowing freely. A gentle beach with the ocean breeze. My mom is all of these. And more!

**Ashley Robinson, Grade: 7**

**Wappingers Falls, NY**

My mentor, my teacher, my angel, my friend. So much more to comprehend. A dove and angel come from above, to teach me to understand and love.

**Cathleen Streicher, Grade: 7**

**Buffalo, NY**

## Ohio

A diamond's beauty. So indescribably complete. Its love inexpressable, so genuinely sweet. Its endless inspiration, and its peaceful, silent grace. Does not even compare to my mom's loving embrace.

**Joree Jacobs, Grade: 7**

**Macedonia, OH**

Mother is a ray of sun on a dark, gloomy day. A cascade of water during droughts of my happiness, and the wind pushing me to succeed.

**Christyn Keyes, Grade: 10**

**Hudson, OH**

Her smile holds the universe. Her eyes hold heaven's gate. Her love is unconditional. My mother is my faith.

**Monica Ross, Grade: 8**

**Dover, OH**

My mom is the underlying rhythm of my heart, a figure of grace I look up to, a secure foothold comforting me and motivating me to press on.

**Andrea Van Deusen, Grade: 10**

**Hudson, OH**

Light as a feather, gentle as a lamb. Brave as a tiger, strong as a ram. Combine all the wonderful things God's given us and you get...Mom.

**Alexandra Zagorski, Grade: 4**

**Solon, OH**

Always thoughtful, always sweet. My mom can't be beat. Always caring, always kind. My mom has an intelligent mind. Always loving, always fair. My mom is very, very rare.

**Jacob Gissinger, Grade: 4**

**Wadsworth, OH**

## Pennsylvania

Her emerald eyes watch over me as I sleep. Although her presence is not visible, her ruby rivers run through me and inspire me. Guardian angel.

**Kate Tejkl, Grade: 10**

**Pittsburgh, PA**

## Texas

My Mom - the guardian angel of my life. Peaceful as a swan on a new crisp morning water. The beautiful sunrise of my morning. My mom. The best.

**Amy Moore, Grade: 5**

**Amarillo,TX**

For her strength when I'm weak. For her compassion when I'm mad. For her wisdom when I'm ignorant. My mom deserves a diamond.

**Ian Ringgenburg, Grade: 7**

**Spring, TX**

Mom deserves a diamond, you see. Just for everything she's done for me. She's loving, caring and willing to lend. But most of all, she is my friend.

**Ryan Stephenson, Grade: 7**

**Arlington, TX**

The apple of my eye. The pink rose in my red garden. The brightest star in the blue night sky. She brightens up my day. Mom, I love you.

**Tami Adams. Grade: 5**

**Joshua, TX**

Churning waves, continuously growing. Life preservers, she's frantically throwing. When I sink, two hands clasp mine. The light fades from view, but she carries me through.

**Abilgail Branch, Grade: 7**

**The Woodlands, TX**

## Utah

Weeping in my mother's arms, I feel a love no one can harm. Her gentle touch, heal my wounds within her clutch.

**Jessica Beus, Grade: 9**

**Sandy, UT**

## Wisconsin

My mom is someone special, exploding with love. She's ravishing and stunning with beauty in her heart. A diamond would represent how much she means to me.

**Michele Helget, Grade: 6**

**Somerset, WI**

## Who Invented Mother's Day?

The person associated with creating Mother's Day is Anna Jarvis. It was first celebrated at Andrews Methodist Church in West Virginia on May 10, 1907, to honor the memory of her own mother who died three years earlier. The church bell rang 72 times for each year of her mother's life. In 1914, President Woodrow Wilson declared Mother's Day a national holiday.

Anna Jarvis was an early reformer of women's rights. She was a teacher in Grafton, West Virginia, cared for her blind sister, was a literary editor, and participated in the temperance and suffrage movements.

Nearly fifty countries honor their mothers with a special day. Although International Mother's Day is May 11, the United States always celebrates this holiday on the second Sunday of May.

**Anna Jarvis**
*"A mother's love is new every day."*

"Seven years after the death of my mother, I woke up suddenly and saw the moon shining brightly. The moon is always expressing something deep, calm, and tender, like the love of a mother for her child. I felt bathed in her love, and realized that my mother is still alive and will always be alive. I few hours earlier, I had seen my mother very clearly in a dream. She was young and beautiful, talking to me, and I talked to her. Since that time, I know that my mother is always with me."

**Cultivating the Mind of Love.    Thich Nhat Hahn.
Permission of Parallax Press, Berkeley, California.**

# *PART THREE*

## *Adoption Resource Network*

*"Another favourite haunt of mine was the orchard, where the fruit ripened early in July...As the joyous breezes flew about the trees the apples tumbled to my feet. Oh, the delight with which I gathered up the fruit in my pinafore, pressed my face against the smooth, cheeks of the apples, still warm from the sun, and skipped back to the house!"*

**Helen Keller. *The Story of My Life.***

# *Adoption Resource Network*

Following is a list of addresses that adoptees, birthparents, and/or adoptive parents may consult for further information. Some addresses may have changed since this publication.

**Support, Search and/or Referral Organizations**

Adoptee - Birthparent Searches (ABC)
234 N. 2nd St.
Jeanette, PA 15644
John Howard, Exec. Officer
(310) 285-6786

Adoptee - Birthparent Support Network (ABSN)
3421 M St. NW, No. 328
Washington, DC 20007
Robyn S. Quinter, Bd. Member
(202) 686-4611

Adoptees' Birthparents' Association
P. O. Box 33
Camarillo, CA 93011
Alberta F. Sorensen, Contact
(805) 482-8667

Adoption Crossroads
74 Lakewood Drive
Congers, NY 10920
845-268-0283
Joe Soll, Director
www.adoptioncrossroads.org

Adoptees In Search (AIS)
P. O. Box 41016
Bethesda, MD 20824
Joanne W. Small MSW, Dir.
(301) 656-8555

Adoption Identity Movement (AIM)
P. O. Box 9783
Grand Rapids, MI 49509
(616) 531-1380

Adoptee's Liberty Movement
Association (ALMA)
P. O. Box 85
Denville, NJ 07834
Marie H. Anderson, Coordinater
973-586-1358
www.almasociety.org

Adoption Resource Network, Inc.
P. O. Box 178
Pittsford, NY 14534
585-586-9586
www.arni.org

American Adoption Congress
P. O. Box 42730
Washington, DC 20015
(202) 483-3399
www.americanadoptioncongress.org

American World War II Orphans
Network (AWON)
910 Princess Anne St.
Fredericksburg, VA 22401
(360) 733-1678
www.awon.org

Bastard Nation
P.O. Box 271672
Houston, TX, 77277
415-704-3166
www.bastards.org

Concerned Persons For Adoption
P. O. Box 179
Whippany, NJ 07981
Janet O'Neill, Pres.
www.cpfanj.org

Concerned United Birthparents, Inc.
P. O. Box 230457
Encinitas,CA 92023
800-822-2777
www.cubirthparents.org

Families For Private Adoption
P. O. Box 6375
Washington, DC 20015
Laurie Mosier, Pres.
(202) 722-0338
www.ffpa.org

Friends In Adoption (FIA)
P. O. Box 659
Auburn, WA 98071-0659
206-264-5136
www.friends-in-adoption.org

Jewish Children's Adoption
Network (JCAN)
P. O. Box 147016
Denver, CO 80214-7016
(303) 573-8113

Latin America Parents
Association (LAPA)
P. O. Box 339-340
Brooklyn NY 11234
(718) 236-8689

National Adoption Center (NAC)
1500 Walnut St. Ste. 701
Philadelphia, PA 19102
Carolyn Johnson, Exec. Dir.
www.adopt.org
(215) 735-9988 (800) TO-ADOPT

National Adoption Information
Clearinghouse (NAIC)
330 C Street, SW
Washington, DC 20447
703-352-3488
www.naic.acf.hhs.gov

National Coalition To End Racism
In America's Child Care System
(NCERACCS)
22075 Koths
Taylor, MI 48180

Carol Coccia, Pres.
(313) 295-0257

PACT – An Adoption Alliance
4179 Piedmont Ave, Suite 330
Oakland, CA 94611
510-243-9460
www.pactadopt.org
Beth Hall, Director

RESOLVE of Northern California
312 Sutter Street, Suite 405
San Francisco, CA 94108
415-788-6772
Ellen Roseman, Adoption Chair
www.resolvenc.org

TRY Resource/ Referral Center
P. O. Box 989
Northampton, MA 01061-0989
www.try.org

**Registries**

Adoption.com
459 N. Gilbert Rd
Gilbert, AZ 85234
480-446-0500
www.adoption.com

Adoptee's Liberty Movement (ALMA)
P. O. Box 85
Denville, NJ 07834
Marie H. Anderson, Coordinater
973-586-1358
www.almasociety.org

International Soundex Reunion
Registry
P.O. Box 2312
Carson City, NV 89702-2312
775-882-7755
www.isrr.net

**Where to Write for Vital Records**

This publication on where to inquire about birth, death, marriage and divorce records is for sale by the U. S. Government Printing Office.

U. S. Department of Health and Human Services
Superintendent of Documents
Mail Stop: SSOP
Washington, DC 20402-9328

**Birth Records and Master Death File**
D. C. Vital Records
800 9th St SW 1st Floor
Washington, D. C 20024
202-783-1809

**U.S. Government Agencies**
Immigration and Naturalization Services (INS)
U.S. Department of Justice
425 I Street NW
Washington, DC 30536
202-514-2000

The National Archives
Washington, DC 20408
202-501-5402

Dept. of State, Passport Agency
1425 K Street NW
Washington, DC 20524
202-647-0518

Social Security Administration
6401 Security Boulevard
Baltimore, MD 21235
410-965-8882

Child Welfare League of America
440 First St. NW. Third Floor
Washington, D.C. 20402
202-638-2952
www.cwla.org

# Bibliography

Adopton.com. Pertman, Adam.

Aigner, Hai J. *Faint Trails*. Paradigm Press. 1980.

American Adoption Congress. www.americanadoptioncongress.org.

Berger, Peter L. *An Invitation to Sociology. – A Humanistic Perspective*. Pelican. 1966.

Brodzinsky, Schecter & Henig. *Being Adopted - The Lifelong Search for Self*. Doubleday. New York. 1992.

Burgess, Linda Cannon. *The Art of Adoption*. Acropolis Books Ltd. 1976.

Clewer, Lisa. *Official ALMA Searcher's Guide for Adults*. 1982. Printed and distributed by Adoptee's Liberty Movement Association.

Culligan, Joseph J. *You, Too, Can Find Anybody. A Reference Manual*. Hallmark Press, Inc. 1993.

-------. *Adoption Searches Made Easier*. FJA, Inc. Miami, FL. 1996.

Darling, David. *Zen Physics: The Science of Death, The Logic of Reincarnation*. 1996. Harper Collins Publishers.

Disney Enterprises. *The Lion King*. 1994.

Fisher, Florence. *The Search for Anna Fisher*. Fawcett Crest. 1973.

Floyd County Chamber of Commerce of New Albany Economics Development Commission. *A Profile of New Albany and Floyd County, Indiana*. 1985.

Gediman, Judith, and Brown,Linda P. *Birth Bond, Reunions Between Birthparents & Adoptees... What Happens After*. 1989. New Horizon Press.

Gohman, James. Floyd County Historical Society. Special Committee. 1994

Gravelle, Karen, and Fischer, Susan. *Where Are My Birth Parents?* Walker and Company. NY. 1993.

Hanh, Thich Nhat. *Cultivating the Mind of Love*. 1996. Parallax Press, Berkeley, California.

-------. *Living Buddha. Living Christ*. 1995. Riverhead Books.

-------. Our Appointment With Life: Discourse on Living Happily in the Present Moment. 1990. Parallax Press, Berkeley, California.

-------. The Heart of the Buddha's Teaching. 1998. Parallax Press, Berkeley, California.

Kaplan, Sharon. The Seven Core Issues of Adoption. From Differences. June 1996.

Keller, Helen. The Story of My Life.

Leitch, David. Family Secrets. A Writer's Search to Find His Past. Delecorte Press. 1984.

Lifton, Betty Jean. Twice Born. McGraw Hill. 1975.

-------. Lost and Found: The Adoption Experience. New York. Harper and Row. 1988.

-------. Journey of the Adopted Self. Basicbooks. New York. 1994.

Lọc, Âu. Bo De Hai. Van Phat Thanh Thanh. 1997.

Melina. Lois Ruskai. Making Sense of Adoption. Harper And Row. 1989.

Paul, Ellen. Adoption Choices. A Guidebook to National and International Adoption Resources. Visible Ink Press. Detroit, MI. 1991.

Roles, Patricia. Saying Goodbye to a Baby. Volume 2-A. A Counselor's Guide to Birthparent Loss and Grief in Adoption. Child Welfare League of America. Washington D.C. 1989.

Sachdev, Paul. Unlocking the Adoption Files. Lexington Books. 1989.

Sagan, Carl. Cosmos. Random House. 1980.

Soll, Joe. Adoption Healing—A Path to Recovery. Adoption Crossroads.

Sorosky, Arthur D, Annette Baran, and Rueben Pannor. The Adoption Triangle. New York. Anchor Press. 1987.

Strauss, Jean A. Birthright. The Guide to Search and Reunion for Adoptees, Birthparents, and Adoptive Parents. Penguin Books. 1994.

Tribune, New Albany. Harvest Homecoming Edition. October, 1981. Pg. 4-A.

USA Today. Peterson, Karen S. August 2003 Article.

Verrier, Nancy Newton. The Primal Wound. Gateway Press, Inc. Baltimore, MD. 1993.

Watson, Michael C. Why Mom Deserves A Diamond™ Anthology Books. Gallery of Diamonds Publishing. Costa Mesa, CA. 1993-2005.

-------. In Search of Mom- Journey of An Adoptee. Gallery of Diamonds Publishing. Costa Mesa, CA. 1998

# *Index*